D1216918

COMPLETE SPEAKER'S

AND

TOASTMASTER'S LIBRARY

Human Interest Stories

COMPLETE SPEAKER'S
AND
TOASTMASTER'S LIBRARY

Human Interest Stories

by Jacob M. Braude

PRENTICE-HALL, INC.

Englewood Cliffs, N.J.

Eighth Printing.....October, 1971

A

Absent-mindedness

1. "Alert?" repeated a congressman when questioned concerning one of his political opponents. "Why he's alert as a Providence bridegroom I heard of the other day. You know how bridegrooms starting off on their honeymoons sometimes forget all about their brides and buy tickets only for themselves? That's what happened to the Providence young man. And when his wife said to him, "Why Tom, you bought only one ticket," he answered without a moment's hesitation, "By Jove, you're right, dear! I'd forgotten myself entirely!"

Accuracy

2. A tourist was visiting New Mexico. While gazing at the dinosaur bones that were everywhere, he met an old Indian who acted as an unofficial guide.

"How old are these bones?" asked the tourist.

"Exactly one hundred million and three years old," was the Indian's reply.

"How can you be so definite?" inquired the tourist.

"Oh, a geologist told me they were one hundred million years old," replied the Indian, "and that was exactly three years ago."

3. A stranger entered the building and asked a boy standing in the lobby, "Can you tell me where Mr. Smith lives?"

The lad smiled and replied pleasantly, "Yes, sir. I'll show you."

Six flights up the boy pointed out a room as that belonging to Mr.

Smith. The man pounded on the door repeatedly and, after no response, commented, "He's not here."

"Oh, no, sir," replied the boy. "Mr. Smith was downstairs waiting in the lobby."

Admiration

4. A young American woman stood before Beethoven's piano in a Vienna museum. Presently she struck off a few discordant notes. "I suppose," she said to the attendant, "that many noted musicians have inspected this instrument."

"Oh, yes," replied the man. "Recently Paderewski was here."

"Paderewski!" exclaimed the visitor. "Certainly he must have played something wonderful."

"On the contrary; he did not feel worthy to touch it."

Advancement

5. After President Coolidge issued his famous "I do not choose to run" statement, he was besieged by reporters seeking a more detailed statement. One, more persistent than his fellows, followed Mr. Coolidge to the door of his library.

"Exactly why don't you want to be President again, Mr. Coolidge?" he asked.

Coolidge turned and looked him squarely in the eye. "Because," he answered, "there's no chance for advancement."

Advertising

6. A man who lives in the suburbs of Los Angeles and who works in the advertising department of a large metropolitan newspaper had never been able to understand the deferential attitude toward him, bordering on awe, of the children in the block. Recently he was walking around the block for a little stroll and came upon a group of boys discussing the newest American satellite which was hurtling through orbital space around the earth. As he paused to say hello to the youngsters, everything suddenly became clear when one of the boys said to him: "Are you really a space salesman?"

7. A man who owned a house on Chicago's fashionable Lake Shore Drive decided he was tired of it and called upon a real estate broker to offer it for sale.

In the following Sunday's *Chicago Tribune* he read the ad the broker had worked up for him. It sounded so good that he reread it to himself. Then he phoned the broker, to whom he said: "I've decided not to sell." "What made you change your mind?" asked the realtor. "That ad of yours," the owner replied. "It convinced me that this was the kind of house I've been looking for all my life."

8. Ignace Paderewski, the talented Polish pianist, arrived in a small Western town about noon one day and decided to take a walk in the afternoon. While strolling he heard a piano and, following the sound, came to a house on which was a sign reading:

MISS JONES. PIANO LESSONS 25¢ AN HOUR

Pausing to listen he heard the young woman trying to play one of Chopin's nocturnes, and not succeeding very well.

Paderewski walked up to the house and knocked. Miss Jones came to the door and recognized him at once. Delighted, she invited him in. He sat down and played the nocturne as only Paderewski could, afterwards spending an hour in correcting her mistakes. Miss Jones thanked him and he departed.

Some months afterward he returned to the same town, and again took the same walk.

He soon came to the home of Miss Jones, and looking at the sign, he read:

MISS JONES. PIANO LESSONS $1.00 AN HOUR
(PUPIL OF PADEREWSKI)

Advice

9. Two Massachusetts state senators got into an angry debate and one told the other he could "go to hell." The man thus consigned called on Governor Coolidge and asked him to do something about it.

Governor Coolidge replied: "I've looked up the law, Senator, and you don't have to go there."

10. A young composer once came to Mozart for advice on how to develop creatively. "Begin writing simple things first," Mozart told him, "songs, for example."

"But you composed symphonies when you were only a child," the man exclaimed.

"Ah," Mozart answered, "but I didn't go to anybody to find out how to become a composer!"

Age

11. Ethel Barrymore was in her dressing room in Hollywood when a studio usher tapped on the door. "A couple of gals in the reception room, Miss Barrymore, who say they went to school with you. What shall I do?"

"Wheel them in," said the incomparable Ethel.

12. At a reception in Washington, a young man was asked by a widow to guess her age. "You must have some idea," she said as he hesitated.

"I have several ideas," he admitted with a smile. "The only trouble is that I hesitate whether to make you ten years younger on account of your looks, or ten years older on account of your brains."

13. Marlene Dietrich saw the first week's rushes of a new picture and complained that they didn't suit her. The cameraman had also photographed her in "The Garden of Allah," one of the star's favorites; so they went to a projection room and had "The Garden of Allah" shown. When it was over Miss Dietrich said, "I looked gorgeous in that picture. Why can't we get the same result in this one?"

"Well, you see, Miss Dietrich," said the cameraman, "I'm eight years older now."

14. Actress Joan Crawford was known to have a good library and to be one of the few actresses who read the classics. The story is told about a celebrated writer whom she was once entertaining and who complimented her on her taste in books.

"You see," said Joan, flattered, "my mother always gives me a book on my birthday."

Here her husband broke in: "You can also see," he said, grinning broadly, "that Joan has a pretty large library!"

Aging

15. Victor Hugo, titan of French literature, was once called upon to comfort a friend who had arrived at his fiftieth birthday and was depressed at the idea of growing old.

"You should rejoice, my friend," Hugo told him, "that you have escaped your forties, which are the old age of youth, and have at last arrived at the age of fifty, which is the youth of old age."

16. It is said that when Konrad Adenauer, former West German Chancellor, was laid up with the grippe, he chafed at his doctor and said he had to get better because he was scheduled to make an official trip abroad.

"I'm not a magician," said the doctor. "I can't make you young again."

To which Adenauer is reported to have replied: "I'm not asking that. I don't want to become young again; all I want is to go on getting old."

Alcoholic Liquor

17. A physician, observing Charles Bannister, the great English actor, about to drink a glass of brandy, said: "Don't drink that filthy stuff; brandy is the worst enemy you have."

"I know that," responded Charles, "but you know we are commanded by scripture to love our enemies."

18. Returning from a trip to Europe, Mark Twain became annoyed as a customs official rummaged through his baggage. "My good friend," the author exclaimed, "you don't have to mix up all my things. There are only clothes in there—nothing but clothes."

But the suspicious fellow kept rooting about until he hit upon something hard. He pulled out a quart of the finest quality bourbon. "You call this 'just clothes'?" cried the official.

"Sure thing," Twain replied calmly. "That is my nightcap."

Alertness

19. A senator telephoned the British Embassy on George Washington's birthday. When the phone was answered, he kidded the embassy staff member: "You are working on one of our national holidays; I'm not sure our government would approve of that."

Replied the Britisher: "My government expects me to be attentive to duty on *all* American holidays. By not being alert one July fourth, we lost some valuable real estate!"

Ambition

20. A young man had determined from boyhood to serve in the ministry. He was handsome, had a brilliant mind, and was a leader in college activities. One of the vice presidents of a large company with offices in his home town had watched the boy's progress during his college years. He offered the young man a good salary to work for the company when he was graduated. The young man declined. The vice president raised the salary offer several times. Still the lad steadfastly insisted that he had other work to do.

Finally the president of the company went to him. "Isn't the salary big enough?" he asked.

"Yes," the young man replied thoughtfully, "the salary is big enough, but the job isn't."

—ANNIE LAURIE VON TUNGELN

America—American—Americanism

21. When Guizot, the famous Frenchman, visited our country in its early days, he asked James Russell Lowell how long he thought the Republic would last. Lowell replied: "Sir, the Republic will last as long as the ideals and principles of the founders remain dominant in the hearts of the people."

22. Years ago, King Carol told Bruce Lockhart how he had selected fourteen of the brightest young men in Rumania for training in the government service. Seven he sent to England, seven to America, to study the economic and political systems. "The seven who went to England were very smart and they all now have important posts in Bucharest."

"What about the seven you sent to America?" asked Lockhart.

"They were even smarter," said the King. "They stayed there."

—LEONARD LYONS

23. In the closing days of the war in Europe, 175 Yank prisoners —Catholic and Protestant—gave Nazi captors a lesson in Americanism.

The word got around that Jewish soldiers in the group of prisoners were to be separated from others and assigned to a special back-breaking labor detail. The boys talked it over; the Jewish soldiers, about 75 in number, urged their buddies not to stick their necks out. The following morning the Kommandant rasped: "Achtung! All prisoners of Jewish blood advance one pace forward." And 250 Americans stepped out!

Anger

24. Abraham Lincoln, on hearing a friend speak angrily of some-one, advised him to sit down and put all his abuse into a letter. "It will do you good," Lincoln said.

When the letter was written it was read to Lincoln, who com-mended it heartily for its severity. The writer was pleased, and asked, "How would you advise me to send it?"

"Send it?" asked Lincoln. "Oh, I wouldn't *send* it. I sometimes write a letter like that—it does *me* good; *but I never send it.*"

25. Sister Elizabeth Kenny, the famed Irish-Australian nurse, was once asked by a friend how she managed to stay constantly cheerful, no matter what the provocation.

Said the friend: "I suppose you were just born calm and smiling."

"Oh no," laughed Sister Kenny. "As a girl my temper often got out of bounds. But one day when I became angry at a friend over some trivial matter, my mother gave me advice that I stored in my mind and have called upon for guidance ever since.

"Mother told me 'Elizabeth, anyone who angers you conquers you.'"

Anonymity

26. A Texas oilman some years ago was participating in a charity drive. At a large banquet he rose to his feet. "Mah name," he said, "is James R. Robinson, and mah nickname is Jimmy. Ah have a ten thousand acre ranch in the Panhandle and mah brand is JR. Ah run ten thousand barrels of oil a day, and ah own outright the Robinson Oil & Gas Company. Ah have a ten thousand dollar baby-blue Cadillac outside and on it, in gold, are mah initials, JRR. Ah like this charity and want to give ten thousand dollars—ahnony-mously!"

Apology—Apologies

27. When Champ Clark was Speaker of the House, Congressman Johnson of Indiana interrupted the speech of an Ohio representative, calling him a jackass. The expression was ruled to be unparliamentary and Johnson apologized.

"I withdraw the unfortunate word, Mr. Speaker, but I insist that the gentleman from Ohio is out of order."

"How am I out of order?" angrily shouted the other.

"Probably a veterinary could tell you," answered Johnson. And this was allowed to enter the record.

28. In the good old days, a king and queen were so fond of their court jester they often had him as their sole dinner guest. On one such occasion, the jester asserted: "An apology can be worse than an insult."

APPEASEMENT

"Either you prove that," remarked the royal host, "or I'll have you beheaded."

After dinner his royal highness happened to bend over. WHAM! The jester landed a lusty kick on the royal pants, then quickly cried: "Pardon me, Sire. I thought you were the Queen."

—ALEX F. OSBORN

Appeasement

29. In his dealings with the Führer, Mr. Chamberlain seemed to think that the saving of a million lives was well worth the surrender of England's honor. His conferences with Hitler at Berchtesgaden and Godesberg read like the diary of a young lady crossing the Atlantic for the first time.

Monday—I feel highly honored at being placed at the Captain's table.

Tuesday—I spent the morning on the bridge with the Captain. He seemed to like me.

Wednesday—The Captain made proposals to me unbecoming an officer and a gentleman.

Thursday—The Captain threatened to sink the ship unless I agreed to his proposals.

Friday—I saved six hundred lives!

—WILLIS H. KINGSLAND

Appreciation

30. As a simple, unpretentious admirer of fine art, Elbert Hubbard derived much pleasure from visiting the great art galleries. One day he was admiring a priceless painting in a New York gallery when a friend chided him: "Elbert, why do you allow yourself to become so enthusiastic over things you can never afford to own?"

"Harry," replied the sage of East Aurora, "I would rather be able to appreciate things I can't have than to have things I am not able to appreciate."

31. In a lecture to a group of Korean officers, an American general took two or three minutes to tell his favorite joke. The interpreter then translated, using only seven or eight words. Nevertheless everyone burst into hearty laughter. After the lecture the general asked the interpreter how he had been able to tell such a long joke so quickly. "Well, sir," confessed the Korean, "I didn't think everyone would get the point so I just said 'The General has just told a joke. Everyone will please laugh.'"

32. A rabbi was once passing through a field where he saw a very old man planting an oak tree.

"Why are you planting that tree?" said he. "You surely don't expect to live long enough to see the acorn grow up into an oak tree?"

"Ah," replied the old man, "my ancestors planted trees not for themselves, but for us, in order that we might enjoy their shade and their fruit. I am doing likewise for those who will come after me."

Armed Forces

33. When Major General Merritt was dealing with Aguinaldo, he sought a conference with Admiral Dewey on the *Olympia*. There was considerable discussion as to jurisdiction. Finally General Merritt said:

"Admiral, how far, in your opinion, does your jurisdiction extend on this island?"

Admiral Dewey took two short turns on the quarterdeck before answering. Then he said:

"General, my jurisdiction extends from as close to shore as I can move these flatirons," pointing to the American fleet, "to as far into the island as I can throw a shell."

34. When the British under Lord Nelson were bearing down to attack the combined fleets off Trafalgar, the first lieutenant of the *Revenge,* on going to see that all hands were at their quarters, observed one of the men kneeling at the side of his gun. So very unusual was this devout attitude that he went and asked the man if he was afraid.

"Afraid?" answered the honest tar, with a countenance expressive of the utmost disdain. "No; I was only praying that the enemy's shot may be distributed in the same proportion as the prize money, the greater part among the officers."

Art—Artist

35. The composer, Maurice Ravel, was an enthusiastic collector of rare books and prints, fine porcelains, and other *objects d'art.* In his study, occupying a place of honor on a pedestal, stood his most treasured possession—a ball of smoked crystal, which he pointed to with great pride.

"Maurice," his guests would whisper in awe, "where did you get it? It's exquisite!"

"You really think so?" he would answer modestly. "Well it's just a burned-out electric bulb."

36. George Bernard Shaw once visited sculptor Jacob Epstein in the latter's studio. As they chatted, Shaw noticed a huge block of stone in a corner of the room.

"What is it for?" he asked.

"I don't know yet," said Epstein. "I'm still making plans."

"You mean you plan your work?" exclaimed Shaw. "You, an artist? Why, I change my mind several times a day!"

"That's all right with a four-ounce manuscript," replied Epstein, "but not with a four-ton block."

Attitude—Attitudes

37. "My mother once sent me to pick a quart of raspberries," reminisced a well-known citizen recently as he let his thoughts stroll back to the days of his boyhood in the country. "I didn't want to pick a quart of raspberries—I wanted to do anything but that. I trudged unwillingly toward the berry patch.

"Then a happy thought came to me: I would pick *two* quarts of berries, and surprise the family! That changed everything. I had such a good time picking those two quarts that I've never forgotten it. I redeemed an undesirable situation by changing an inner attitude."

Authorship

38. Thomas Mann always worked on each book for a very long time. Even when the manuscript supposedly was ready, he continued to work on it. When he kept changing things in *The Magic Mountain*, his publisher finally called him up and wailed, "We'll never get this book out! You've been working on it for eternity!"

"After all," was Mann's calm reply, "I'm writing it for eternity!"

39. Nathaniel Hawthorne, having lost his government position, went home, dejected and almost desperate. His wife, after a time, learning the reason for his gloom, instead of giving way to reproaches, set pen and ink on the table and, lighting a fire in the grate, put her arms about his shoulders and said, "Now you will be able to write your book."

He took heart and the world was enriched with *The Scarlet Letter*.

40. Novelist Sinclair Lewis was to lecture a group of college students who planned literary careers. Lewis opened his talk by asking: "How many of you really intend to be writers?"

All hands went up.

"In that case," said Lewis, returning his notes to his pocket, "my advice to you is to go home and write."

With that, he left the room.

41. Seven times a persistent young playwright brought to Charles Frohman an impossible farce, slightly rewritten after each submission, and seven times the celebrated producer rejected it.

"Once and for all, the play won't do!" Frohman stormed. "There is no need showing it to me again!"

"But isn't there some way you can put it on the stage?" the playwright pleaded.

Frohman reflected a moment. "There is one way," he admitted, "but you wouldn't care for it."

"Oh, I'd submit to anything to get my play on the stage!" the eager playwright declared.

"Very well, then," said Frohman. "We'll just grind it up and use it as a snowstorm."

B

Bachelorhood

42. An old man was talking to a bachelor and asked him why he did not marry. The bachelor parried the question by telling about the different young women he had known, finding some fault with each one. But it appeared that all of them had succeeded in getting married.

"You're in danger of getting left," said the old man. "You'd better hurry up before it's too late."

"Oh," said the bachelor, "there are just as many good fish left in the sea."

"That may be true," replied the old man, "but the bait—isn't there danger of the bait becoming stale?"

43. The bachelor's attractive new housekeeper tiptoed into the study and asked apologetically, "Sir, shall I clean your stove and sweep your porch now?"

"Margie," said the bachelor, "in this house we are all for one and one for all. You do not say 'your stove' or 'your porch' or 'your chair.' Instead you say 'our stove' or 'our porch' or 'our chair.'"

That evening Margie served a splendid dinner to the bachelor and his boss and the boss' daughter, whom the bachelor was anxious to impress.

Margie was late in serving the last course and she rushed into the dining room and excitedly announced: "I'm sorry I was late, sir, but I was upstairs chasing a mouse from under 'our bed.'"

Beauty

44. Two businessmen were relaxing on the beach at Miami. "You know," one began, "what does everyone see in Elizabeth Tayor? Take away her hair, her lips, her eyes, and her figure—and what've you got?" The other businessman grunted. "My wife," he said sadly.

45. At dinner one night, Chauncey Depew joined a small group of friends who were in the midst of an animated discussion. "Oh, Mr.

Depew!" exclaimed one of the ladies, "you're just in time to settle an argument. What is the most beautiful thing in the world?"

"A beautiful woman," replied the gallant Depew, without hesitation.

But his companion seemed shocked at his levity. "I contend," she said, seriously, "that sleep is the most beautiful."

"Well," said Depew thoughtfully, "next to a beautiful woman, sleep is!"

—ALAN GRAY M. CAMPBELL

Begging

46. The kindly old lady was much impressed with the street beggar. "You poor man!" she exclaimed. "It must be dreadful to be lame. But you know it could be worse. It would be much worse if you were blind!"

"You're tellin' *me*, lady," responded the beggar. "When I was blind, people was all a-time givin' me foreign coins."

Behavior

47. One day when Al Smith was showing a group of women through his Empire State Building, and they were zooming up the hundred floors in the elevator, one of the women said, "Mr. Smith, if the cable in this elevator should break, would I go up or down?" And Al replied: "Lady, that all depends on the kind of life you've lived."

48. A man from Milwaukee went into the washroom of the Union Station in Chicago, and was amazed to notice how spic and span everything was, and that a number of people seemed to be leaving very quickly. He wondered what had caused all this activity and tension, until he looked up and saw a sign on the wall reading "You are now on T.V."

Benevolence

49. The usual crowd of small boys was gathered about the entrance of a circus tent in a small town, pushing each other and trying to get a glimpse of the interior. A man standing near by watched them for a few minutes, then walking up to the ticket-taker he said with an air of authority:

"Let these boys in, and count them as they pass." The gateman did as requested, and when the last lad had gone in, he turned and said: "Twenty-eight, sir."

"Good," said the man, smiling as he walked away. "I thought I guessed right."

Bible, The

50. A Mohammedan trader in India once asked a European whether he could not obtain a *Bible* for him. "What for?" asked the European in surprise. "You wouldn't be able to read it."

"True," replied the Mohammedan. "What I want is a European *Bible.*"

Then the European asked, "What would you do with it?"

"Well, when a ship brings a trader who is unknown to me and who wishes to trade with me, I'll put the *Bible* in his way and watch him. If he opens it and reads it, I will know that I can trust him, but if he brushes it aside with a sneer or even a curse, I will have nothing to do with him because I will know that I cannot trust him."

51. When John Wanamaker was eleven years old, he bought a *Bible.* In later years he said of this purchase: "I have, of course, made large purchases of property in my time, involving millions of dollars, but it was as a boy in the country, when I was eleven, that I made my greatest purchase. In the little mission Sunday school I bought a small red leather *Bible* for $2.75, which I paid for in small installments. Looking back over my life I see that that little red book was the foundation on which my life has been built, and the thing which has made possible all that has counted in my life. I know now that it was the greatest investment and the most important and far-reaching purchase I ever made."

Birthday—Birthdays

52. Ethel Barrymore once invited friends to a birthday party. "There'll be a birthday cake, I suppose?" someone asked.

"Yes, there'll be a birthday cake, never fear," Miss Barrymore replied.

"And candles, of course?"

"My friend," said Miss Barrymore, "it's to be a birthday party, not a torchlight procession."

53. A young man was deeply in love with a beautiful girl. One day she told him that the next day would be her birthday, and he laughingly said he would send her a bunch of roses, one for each year of her life.

That evening he wrote to his florist, ordering twenty-four roses to be sent to the young lady on the first delivery the following day.

The proprietor of the flower shop, looking over the mail in the morning, said to his salesman:

"Tom, here's an order from young Mr. Higgins for twenty-four roses. He's a mighty good customer; let's give him a break and put in an extra dozen."

And the young man never did find out what made the young lady so angry with him.

Blame

54. An editor had to admonish his son because of the lad's truancy from school and general lack of diligence.

"You must go every day, study hard, and become a really good scholar," said the father. "Otherwise, you know, you'll never follow in my footsteps and become an editor. Knowledge is important. What would you do, for instance, if your magazine came out full of mistakes?"

"Father," said the boy, "I'd blame the printer."

And the father went away happily, knowing that he had a successor.

55. A man answered his doorbell and a friend walked in, followed by a big, shaggy dog. As they sat talking, the dog bumped into an end-table, sending a lamp crashing to the floor. Then he chewed on the rug for a while. Restlessly he roamed through the house, his progress marked by crashes and tinkling glass. Then he jumped upon the sofa, with his muddy feet, and curled up for a nap.

The outraged householder, unable to contain himself any longer, burst out, "Don't you think you should train your dog better?"

"My dog!" exclaimed the friend, surprised. "I thought it was your dog!"

Business Enterprise

56. George Eastman, captain of Kodak, had always had a genius for detail. Some years ago, after looking over the architect's plan for a theatre with 6,000 seats which he was planning to give to the city of Rochester, Mr. Eastman indicated general approval, but thought there was room for two more seats in the orchestra.

"Why raise the issue about two seats when there are to be 6,000 in the theatre?" queried the architect.

And Mr. Eastman is reported to have replied: "Each extra seat, for which there is ample room, would bring in an additional revenue of 30¢ a show, making 60¢ for the day, or $3.60 a week, figuring six performances. At the end of the year the revenue would amount to $187.20, which, incidentally, is the interest on $3,120 for a year."

C

Cause and Effect

57. George Bernard Shaw, tall and slender, was once told by G. K. Chesterton, who was noted for his rotundity:

"To look at you, Shaw, a person would think there was a famine in England."

To which Shaw sarcastically retorted: "Yes, and to look at you, he'd think you were the cause of it."

58. Lawrence Kimpton, when Chancellor of the University of Chicago, told an audience of the time he was playing host to a visiting foreign scientist. In preparation for the day when they would be visiting the State of New York and seeing the great Niagara Falls, Chancellor Kimpton took the time to acquire a mass of facts and data concerning the great waterfall and was prepared to entertain and amaze his guest with interesting and unusual information.

Approaching the scene and watching the great cascade, the Chancellor remarked to his guest:

"Do you realize that approximately 4,534,288 gallons of water go over those falls every minute?"

"Sure, and what's to prevent it?" was the visiting scientist's casual reply.

59. A teacher while conducting a class said to her pupils: "Now we have fifteen minutes within which to do nothing else, so let's work some riddles and conundrums. I'll ask the first. Let's see who can guess the answer. 'If Washington crossed the Delaware, how old am I?'"

There was a blank stare on everyone's face, but for one little youngster in the back of the room who was busily scribbling on a piece of paper. Finally, he raised his hand and said:

"Teacher, I have the answer."

"What is it, Johnny," said she.

"Forty-eight," came back the answer.

"That's right, but how did you guess it?"

"Oh," said Johnny, "I didn't guess it, I worked it out by arithmetic; you see, we have a brother at home, his name is Tommy, he's twenty-four, and he's half nuts. Two times twenty-four is forty-eight."

Caution

60. A Minneapolis teacher gave $500 to a charming gyp for a half interest in a mythical training school—and then the man skipped town and couldn't be found.

When she went to the Better Business Bureau with her tale of woe, the Bureau man asked: "Why didn't you investigate first? Didn't you know about our service?"

"Oh, yes, I've known about the Bureau for years," she answered. "But I was afraid you'd tell me not to do it!"

—Frank W. Brock

61. A farmer whose corn crop hadn't done well decided to "borrow" from his prosperous neighbor's field. With a large sack tucked under his arm, and his small son dogging his footsteps, he hurried to a distant corner of the field.

On arrival, he peered cautiously to the left, to the right, ahead and behind, to make sure he was not observed.

Just as he reached out a hand to pluck the first ear of corn, the lad spoke: "Daddy," he reminded, "you didn't look up!"

—Ruth A. Pray

Character

62. A man in Boston was very angry about an article which defamed his character. He went to Dr. Everett and asked his advice as to what he should do about it.

"Nothing," said Dr. Everett. "Half the people who got the paper never saw the article. Half who read it did not understand it. Half who did understand it did not believe it. Half of those who believed it were of no importance anyway."

63. A scorpion, being a very poor swimmer, asked a turtle to carry him on his back across a river. "Are you mad?" exclaimed the turtle. "You'll sting me while I'm swimming and I'll drown."

"My dear turtle," laughed the scorpion, "if I were to sting you, you would drown and I would go down with you. Now where is the logic in that?"

"You're right!" cried the turtle. "Hop on!" The scorpion climbed aboard and halfway across the river gave the turtle a mighty sting. As they both sank to the bottom, the turtle resignedly said:

"Do you mind if I ask you something? You said there'd be no logic in your stinging me. Why did you do it?"

"It has nothing to do with logic," the drowning scorpion sadly replied. "It's just my character."

Charity

64. George Bernard Shaw, doing his duty at a benefit affair, asked a dowager to dance. As they waltzed, she simpered, "Oh, Mr. Shaw, whatever made you ask poor little me to dance?" Replied the gallant G.B.S., "This is a charity ball, isn't it?"

65. The preacher, after talking to his congregation about free salvation, asked Brother Smith to take up the collection. A parishioner got to his feet and protested: "Parson, I thought you said salvation was free—free as the water we drink."

"Salvation is free, Brother," replied the minister. "It's free and the water is free, but when we pipe it to you, you have to pay for the piping."

Choice

66. A story is told in Benjamin Franklin's autobiography of a clergyman ordered to read the proclamation issued by Charles I, bidding the people to return to sports on Sunday. To the congregation's amazement and horror, he did read the royal edict in church, which many clergy had refused to do. But he followed it with the words, "Remember the Sabbath day to keep it holy," and added, "Brethren, I have laid before you the commandment of your king and the commandment of your God. I leave it to you to judge which of the two ought rather to be observed."

—W. J. ISBELL

Church Affiliation

67. A businessman was interviewing a job applicant. "Now then," he stated briskly, "for this position we need a real live wire. But, at the same time, he must be methodical. I can't overemphasize the importance of his being methodical."

"Hmm," the applicant said after some thought, "if that's the case, I guess I don't want the job after all."

"No? Why not?"

"Well," replied the applicant, "it's that 'methodical.' All my life I've been a good Presbyterian, and I don't believe that I'm going to change now."

Church Attendance

68. Two men were watching their church burn down. Said one to the other: "Bill, I haven't seen you at church for a long time. Why don't you come more often?"

To which Bill replied: "This is the first time I've seen the church on fire."

69. A minister met an unregenerate acquaintance on the street and inquired, during their brief conversation, "Just what do you have against coming to church?"

"Plenty!" snarled the sinner. "The first time I went, they threw water in my face, and the second time they tied me to a woman I've had to support ever since."

"I see," said the minister quietly, "and the next time they'll throw dirt on you."

70. A pastor tried to persuade a certain man to join the church. The man said, "Why should I join the church? I can worship in the beauty of nature by myself. I can read my *Bible* and say my prayers. I can follow the teachings of Christ without the help of anyone else."

The two men were standing in a room. Nearby, glowing coals lay in the fireplace. The minister was silent. Then he went to the fireplace, took a tong, lifted a glowing ember from the remaining coals. Carefully, he laid it on the apron away from the other coals. Within a few minutes, as they watched, the glowing coal became a blackened ember. The man said quietly, "I see what you mean."

Church Collections

71. The minister walked into the vestry and was shocked to discover his wife with both hands in the collection plate.

"Ethel," he shouted, "what in the world do you think you're doing?"

His wife replied, "I'm looking for a button to sew on your coat."

72. When Andrew Carnegie once visited a small church in Georgia he dropped into the collection plate a $50 bank note. The old man passing the plate was startled and took the plate to the minister, pointing out the note. The minister expressed amazement and examined the note on both sides. Shaking his head, he proceeded to count the change in the plate.

"Friends, the Lord has been mighty good to us today," he told the congregation. "The collection amounts to $6.60, and if the bill that the gentleman with the gray hair and beard has given us is good, we have $56.60. Let us give thanks, put our trust in the Lord, and pray that it may be a good bill."

Citizenship

73. A man was giving a government clerk information for filling out a required form. When the clerk came to "Nationality" he said, "You're French, aren't you?"

"No, English," replied the citizen. "Both my father and mother are English."

"But you were born in France," protested the clerk.

"What's that got to do with it?" demanded the exasperated citizen. "If your dog had puppies in a stable, you wouldn't call them horses."

Club Membership

74. A new pastor was invited by the local Kiwanians to join their club. The membership secretary reminded him, however, that it was the rule of the club to have only one representative from each profession and that they already had one for the category of pastor. The only profession not represented at the moment was that of hog caller. Would the pastor mind? "Well," was the reverend gentleman's reply, "where I come from I was known as the shepherd, but of course you know your group best."

College

75. The self-made storekeeper had little patience with formal education. When a young man applied for work in his store, the owner said: "Sure, I'll give you a job. Sweep up the store."

"But I'm a college graduate," protested the young man.

"Okay, I'll show you how."

76. One day an Eastern university professor visited the expanding campus of the University of California at Los Angeles. He watched construction work on half a dozen new buildings. He inspected new laboratories and attended summer classes in modern study rooms. With one of the deans he walked across miles of eucalyptus-lined lawns and athletic fields. He was impressed.

"My," he said, "just how many students do you have here?"

"Let me see," the dean answered thoughtfully, "I'd say about one in a hundred."

77. Charles W. Eliot, famous president of Harvard University, while being honored one night by a group of educators, made use of the following "reverse process."

"Permit me to congratulate you on the miracles you have performed at the University," remarked one educator. "Since you became president, Harvard has become a storehouse of knowledge."

"That is true," laughed Eliot, "but I scarcely deserve the credit for that. It is simply that the freshmen bring so much knowledge in, and the seniors take so little out."

Communism

78. Asked the first Russian: "What was the nationality of Adam and Eve?"

"There's no doubt that they were Soviet citizens," replied the second. "They had nothing to wear, nothing to eat but an apple, and lived in paradise."

79. An excited supporter burst into the private chambers of the old tiger Clemenceau one day and cried, "Your son has just joined the Communist party." Clemenceau regarded his visitor calmly and remarked, "Monsieur, my son is twenty-two years old. If he had not become a Communist at twenty-two, I would have disowned him. If he is *still* a Communist at thirty, I will do it then."

80. A small Russian boy was asked by his teacher, "What is the size of the Communist Party?"

"About five feet two inches," he promptly replied.

"Idiot!" exploded the teacher. "I mean how many members does it have? How do you get five feet two inches?"

"Well," replied the boy, "my father is six feet tall and every night he puts his hand to his chin and says, 'I've *had* the Communist Party, up to here!'"

Competition

81. An Englishman once migrated to New York where he set himself up in business and put a sign above the door of his establishment reading "Established 1875" and rather prided himself upon the antiquity of his organization. The next day his American rival across the street burlesqued the Englishman's sign by putting up his own sign which read as follows: "Established Yesterday. No Old Goods on Hand."

Complement—Complementary

82. The following advertisement appeared in a New York paper:

> A gentleman who has lost his right leg
> is desirous of making the acquaintance
> of someone who has lost his left leg, in
> order to become associated with him in
> the purchase of boots and shoes, size 8.

A French newspaper editor commenting on the above had this to say: "An American may occasionally lose a leg, but he never loses his head."

Compliment—Compliments—Complimentary

83. In their early and less opulent days, George Burns wanted to send some flowers to Gracie Allen, who was in the hospital. Having exactly enough money to buy eleven roses, he wrote, "Dear Gracie, here are eleven roses. The twelfth one is you."

Compromise—Compromises

84. Carroll R. Harding, president of The Pullman Company, used to tell this story about the naming of the town of Pullman, Illinois.

During the early part of 1880, The Pullman Company purchased more than 4,000 acres of prairie land adjoining Lake Calumet, some twelve miles south of the business district of Chicago. On this tract were constructed shops and a town to house 8,500 people.

Solon Spencer Beman, a New York architect, was the master builder of the model town, which was completed in 1884. As the town was nearing completion, Beman was so proud of his new city with public buildings, residences, paved streets, parks, playgrounds, sewage system, and water supply, that he went to Mr. Pullman and suggested that it would be quite appropriate to name the city "Beman," after its architect.

Mr. Pullman readily admitted that Beman was a pretty name, but said, "Beman, I'll compromise with you. We'll use the first syllable of my name and the second syllable of your name. The city will be called 'Pullman.'"

Conceit

85. When Napoleon visited the members of the French Academy, one of the scientists asked him, "Who do you think, Sire, was the greatest military leader in history?"

"Well," Napoleon said, "I should say that Julius Caesar was the second greatest!"

86. Sir Herbert Beerbohm Tree, British actor and manager, once berated a young actor for his overbearing conceit.

"I assure you, sir," said the other indignantly, "that I am not suffering from a swelled head."

"It isn't the swelling that causes suffering," retorted Tree. "It's the subsequent shrinkage that hurts."

Conformity

87. A lecturer of some renown was asked to speak at a nudist camp. He was greeted by ladies and gentlemen with no more on than nature saw fit to bestow upon them. They suggested that he would probably like to get ready for dinner. He went upstairs, realizing that he must disrobe like the rest of them. He paced the floor in an agonized panic of indecision. The dinner bell rang. With the courage of utter desperation he stripped, and in Adamite splendor descended the staircase—only to find that all the guests had put on evening clothes to do him honor.

—DONALD CULROSS PEATTIE

Context, Out of

88. A sedate English literary man was interviewed by reporters on his arrival in New York. He remembered that he had been warned before leaving London that American newshawks probably would try to make a fool of him.

"Are you going to visit any night clubs during your stay in New York?" was the first question asked.

"Are there any night clubs in New York?" parried the literary man.

The next day he opened his morning paper to an account of the interview. According to the story, the first question he had asked on stepping ashore was: "Are there any night clubs in New York?"

Cooperation

89. A very nice looking young lady walked into a sporting goods store and ordered all the equipment necessary for a baseball game, including a baseball, a bat, a catcher's mitt, and a catcher's mask.

"Are you sure you want all these?" asked the salesman.

The girl nodded. "Yes, I do. My boss said if I'd play ball with him we'd get along fine."

90. It must have been an exciting moment. The two mountain climbers, Edmund Hillary and his guide, Tenzing Norgay, were descending from the peak of Mount Everest, the world's tallest mountain. Suddenly Hillary's feet gave way and he fell downward into a crevasse.

"Tenzing! Tenzing!" he shouted. The guide saw his companion's predicament and instantly went into action. He dug his ax into the ice and held the rope tight. He was able to stop Hillary's fall fifteen feet below. Then, inch by inch, he pulled the fallen climber to safety.

When they arrived in camp, Hillary told the rest of the party how his guide had saved his life. But Tenzing refused any credit. He shrugged off the experience by saying, "Climbers always help each other."

Not only did Hillary owe his life to Tenzing, but his success as well. It was these two men who, in May, 1953, conquered Mount Everest for the first time in history. They alone stood on the "top of the world" and planted the flag of victory. But they could not have done it without the help of each other. Hillary, a New Zealander, was one of the leaders of the expedition. Intelligent and capable, he knew mountains. But little Tenzing, a Sherpa tribesman from Nepal, knew Mount Everest. He knew its crevasses, its best campsites, its peaks. Without him, Hillary would never have reached the top.

—GLYN EVANS

Courage

91. When President Teddy Roosevelt was touring Oklahoma, he drove by to see his old friend, Quanah Parker, chief of the Comanches, who lived twelve miles from Fort Sill. With pride Parker showed Teddy the house he lived in, the white man's clothes he wore, and his children who attended the white man's school.

"See here, Chief," Teddy said, "why don't you set your people a still better example of obeying the laws of the land and the customs of the whites? A white man has only one wife, and here you are living with five squaws. Why don't you give up four of them and remain faithful to the fifth? Then you would really be living as the white man lives."

Parker considered the proposition. "You are my great white father," he said, "and I will do as you wish, on one condition. You pick out the one I am to live with—and then you go tell the other four."

Cover-Up

92. When the drone of airplanes sounded over Germany's ancient town of Freiburg the night of May 10, 1940, scarcely a burgher looked up. Their city was, they knew, of no military significance.

Suddenly bombs whistled down. Freiburg's picturesque "old city" was heavily damaged. Next day Adolf Hitler screamed that the Allies had violated an agreement to spare open cities. He vowed: "Five German bombs will fall for every enemy bomb," and tried to live up to it.

Nazi planes wiped out Rotterdam, swept across the channel to pulverize Dover and Portsmouth and leave London's inner "City" and the cathedral city of Coventry in flaming rubble. The words "blitz" and "total war" were added to military language.

Now, after prolonged insistence by the Western Allies who said none of their planes was near Freiburg that fateful night, the truth has emerged. German officials, digging into the archives of the Institute for Current History, at Munich, found that the bombers that hit Freiburg were German. Field Marshall Hermann Göring had ordered them from Landsburg for a raid on Dijon, France. Lost in heavy clouds, Göring's bombers had dumped their load on Freiburg by mistake. Göring and Hitler agreed to cover up the facts and used the incident to help "justify" the ruthless Nazi invasion of the Low Countries.

Criticism

93. When Walter Winchell was barred on first-night openings from all the Schubert theatres because of his scurrilous criticisms, he said he would go to their closings by waiting a few days.

94. Once, when a young musician's concert was poorly received by the critics, Sibelius patted him gently on the shoulder. "Remember, son," he consoled the young man, "there is no city anywhere in the world where they have erected a statue to a critic."

95. After an execrable performance of *Hamlet* in a small city, the morning newspaper critic wrote:
"There has long been a controversy over the question as to whether Bacon or Shakespeare wrote Shakespeare's plays. I propose we settle it today by opening their graves. Whichever turns over wrote *Hamlet*."

96. Sir Lewis Morris was complaining to Oscar Wilde about the neglect of his poems by the press.

"It is a complete conspiracy of silence against me," said Morris, "a complete conspiracy of silence. What do you suggest I do, Oscar?"

"Join it," said Wilde without much hesitation.

97. Carl Sandburg was persuaded to attend the dress rehearsal of a very serious play by a very serious young dramatist, but unfortunately Sandburg slept through the greater part of the performance. The outraged dramatist chided him later, "How could you sleep when you knew how much I wanted your opinion?"

"Young man," Sandburg reminded him, "sleep *is* an opinion."

D

Dancing

98. A man who was a stranger in town was taken to a dance at a deaf and dumb hospital by a doctor friend of his.

"But how on earth can I ask a deaf and dumb girl to dance?" he asked.

"Just smile and bow to her," explained the doctor, who had done it before.

So the young man picked out a pretty girl, smiled and bowed to her, and away they danced. They danced not only one dance but three, and he was on the point of asking her for another dance when a strange man approached and said lovingly to the girl: "Darling, when are we going to have another dance? It's been over an hour since I danced with you."

"I don't know, dear," said the girl tenderly. "I don't know how to get away from this deaf and dumb idiot!"

Debtor—Creditor

99. One day Jo Davidson, the sculptor, handed me a check, saying, "I thought you might need it." I did need it badly, and having some prospects of repaying it, I accepted. Jo went on, "In my struggling days in Paris, a rich friend financed me for a year. A long time afterward, when I had plenty of money, I invited him to lunch and he brought up the question of the debt. I said, 'No sir, I have no intention of paying you. I have passed on many times that amount to struggling youngsters. Loans to young artists should not be repaid— they should be passed on.'" Jo paused and looked at me. "Orrick, you can do the same with this money!"

—ORRICK JOHNS

100. The celebrated French poet, Saint-Foix, who, in spite of his large income, was always in debt, sat one day in a barber shop waiting to be shaved. He was lathered, and a tradesman entered who happened to be one of the poet's largest creditors. No sooner did he see Saint-Foix than he angrily demanded his money. The poet composedly begged him not to make a scene. "Won't you wait for the money until I am shaved?"

"Certainly," said the other, pleased at the prospect.

Saint-Foix then made the barber a witness to the agreement, took a towel, wiped the lather from his face, and left the shop. He wore a beard until the end of his days.

Decision—Decisions

101. When War Mobilizer James F. Byrnes submitted his resignation to President Roosevelt, he told the press this story to illustrate how he felt:

"A South Carolina farmer hired a man to dig post-holes. The fellow cleaned up the job in jig time, came back next day and cleared stumps in record time.

"The third day the farmer rewarded him with an easy job—sorting good and bad potatoes. After about three hours the chap fainted. Revived, he exclaimed: 'Oh, the job was easy enough—but those damn decisions just mowed me down!'"

Destination

102. The average man's life consists of twenty years of having his mother ask him where he is going; forty years of having his wife ask the same question; and at the end, the mourners wondering, too.

103. A man "butted in" at a waiting line before a ticket window in New York and the men who had been standing in line and who were also in a hurry, glowered.

"I want a ticket for Boston," said the line-crasher, putting fifty cents under the wicket.

"You can't go to Boston for fifty cents," returned the ticket agent.

"Well, then," asked the man, "where can I go for fifty cents?"

And each of the fourteen men in that waiting line quickly told him.

Diagnosis

104. "Doctor, what is wrong with me?"

"Madame, you are too fat, you use too much rouge and lipstick, you get your hair bleached, you smoke too much, and one other thing— you are in the wrong office. The doctor is next door. I am nothing but a newspaperman."

105. A lady with a pain in her side went to see a physician. He told her she had appendicitis and must have an operation. She disliked this diagnosis so she went to another doctor. He told her she had gall bladder trouble and must have an operation. "Where do you go from here?" inquired a friend.

"Back to the first," she declared. "I'd rather have appendicitis."

Dictatorship

106. When Clement Attlee visited Yugoslavia, Tito took him to see the sights and feted his party with feasting and drinking. He kept asking what Attlee thought about Yugoslavia and its program.

"I am much impressed with your progress," Attlee replied finally, "but I am much disturbed because I have not met my counterpart in Yugoslavia—the leader of the opposition."

107. Adolf Hitler was once described as suffering from deep melancholia, arising from a pronounced inferiority complex. After getting unsatisfactory results from many Aryan psychiatrists, he finally was persuaded to consult a distinguished Jewish psychiatrist. After a complete diagnosis, he advised Hitler to repeat constantly to himself: "I am important; I am significant; I am indispensable." Whereupon Hitler shouted: "That is bad advice." When the psychiatrist inquired why, Hitler replied: "I never believe a word I say."

Difference—Differences

108. Paderewski, the late famous pianist, once praised a young polo player for his clever playing.

The young man replied modestly that it was quite different, indeed, from a performance by Paderewski.

"Oh, the difference between us is perfectly clear," answered Pade-rewski. "You are a dear soul who plays polo, while I am a poor Pole who plays solo."

Diplomacy

109. When Joseph Choate was United States ambassador to Great Britain, many amusing incidents arose. For one, he had gained quite a lot of weight while in England. When he returned to this country, some of his friends, remembering his slight build, remarked about his corpulence. "Why, Mr. Choate," said one, "you have been getting stout since you went abroad." "Oh, yes," replied he, "I found it necessary to meet the Englishman half way."

110. Georges Clemenceau, "the Tiger of France," was riding to the Versailles peace conference, and his young secretary was complaining about all the diplomatic baloney.

"It's nothing but a lot of hot air," grumbled the assistant as their car rolled along the Paris streets.

"All etiquette is hot air," answered the premier, "but that's what's in our automobile tires and see how it eases the bumps."

—John Taylor

Disappointment—Disappointments—Disappointing

111. A teen-ager saw an advertisement for "A valuable book, including information every young girl should know before she marries, with full instructions and illustrations." She sent for the volume and received—a cook book.

112. The wife of the poet Louis Untermeyer delights in telling this about her talented spouse: "We went to a costume party one night. Louis was looking his silliest in a paper hat, tooting a horn for nobody's particular benefit, when a young college girl walked up to him, looked him up and down and turned on her heel with: "Huh! And you're Required Reading!"

—Neal O'Hara

Discouragement

113. The oldest member of the town's planning committee had quietly pointed out flaws in several ambitious plans set forth by the Big Thinkers in the group.

"Blast it, Ben," said one firmly, "do you have to throw cold water on everything?"

"Cold water," countered Uncle Ben, "just naturally results when a lot of hot air gets on thin ice!"

Doctor—Patient

114. A doctor in a clinic was interviewing a new patient. "If I find an operation necessary," he asked, "would you have the money to pay for it?"

"Listen, Doc," replied the man, "if I didn't have the money, would you find the operation necessary?"

—Harry Hershfield

115. Johnny Patterson, the famous Irish clown, lay critically ill. The doctor, having done all he could, closed his medicine case and prepared to leave.

"I'll see you in the morning, Johnny," he said cheerfully.

Instinctively, the dying clown smirked and gave his eye a professional roll that had helped launch many a quip.

"Sure, Doc," he murmured, "but will I see you?"

116. "Well, I can find nothing organically wrong with you," said the doctor as he started to put his instruments back into his bag. "As you know, many illnesses come from worry. You probably have some business or social problem that you should talk over with a good psychiatrist. I had a case very similar to yours only a few weeks ago. The man had a $5,000 promissory note to meet in a few days. He didn't see how he was going to be able to get the money to discharge his obligation and, in consequence, worried himself into a state of nervous exhaustion."

"And did you cure him?" asked the patient hopefully.

"Yes, I did," said the doctor. "I told him he must stop worrying; that life is too short to make oneself sick over a scrap of paper. Now he's back to his normal self again and has stopped worrying entirely."

"You said it, man," muttered the patient dejectedly. "I'm the one who loaned him the $5,000."

Drinking

117. Sir William Osler was lecturing one day to a group of medical students on the subject of intoxicating beverages.

"Is it true," asked one of his students, "that alcohol makes people able to do things better?"

"Not at all," replied the famous doctor. "It just makes them less ashamed of doing them badly."

118. There were numerous rumors that General Grant drank too much, and a delegation of Congressmen was appointed to find out the truth.

"Is it true," they asked him, "that you drink to excess?"

"To *what?*" asked Grant.

"To excess," said the leader of the delegation.

"Well, why not?" said Grant. "I just happen to have a bottle around, and if you don't mind taking it 'neat,' let's all have a pull at it. Gentlemen—to excess!"

119. A reader wrote to Dr. Theodore R. Van Dellen, author of the column "How to Keep Well," in the *Chicago Tribune:* "Because of a serious internal condition, I cannot drink alcoholic beverages. Consequently I cannot get that high feeling that makes a person more daring and aggressive. Is there any other way to get it, or some facsimile thereof?" To which the wise doctor replied: "Just act silly, and no one will know the difference. You will feel 'high' the next morning, whereas those who indulged will be feeling mighty low."

Duty—Duties

120. A farmer was walking over his farm with a friend, exhibiting his crops, herds of cattle, and flocks of sheep. His friend was greatly impressed, especially with the splendid sheep. He had seen the same breed before, but never had seen such fine specimens. With great earnestness he asked the farmer how he had succeeded in rearing such fine sheep. The simple answer was, "I take care of my lambs."

121. Someone tells the story about the time a rider who headed a hunting party in England commanded a boy at the gate to open it.

"I'm sorry, sir," answered the boy, "but my father sent me to say that you must not hunt on his grounds."

"Do you know who I am?" demanded the man gruffly.

"No, sir," answered the boy.

"I am the Duke of Wellington."

The boy took off his cap, but he did not open the gate. "The Duke of Wellington will not ask me to disobey my father's orders," he said quietly.

Slowly the man took off his hat, and smiled. "I honor the boy who is faithful to his duty," said the great man, and with that he and his party rode away.

—Nashua Cavalier

E

Economy

122. The wife of a young engineer, off on a job in Iceland, knitted him a warm jacket which she air-mailed with the following letter: "Postage costs so much for every little ounce that I have cut off the buttons. Love and kisses.

"P.S. The buttons are in the right-hand pocket."

123. A father who had been finding it rather expensive keeping a popular son in high school, returned home one evening to be met at the door by his wife.

Beaming broadly, she gave him a quick kiss and then burst out, "I can't wait to tell you, dear! You know those economy lessons you've been giving Junior? Well, they're finally beginning to bear fruit! He told me today what he wants for his birthday—and it will cost only seventy-five cents!"

"Well, well!" beamed the delighted father. "And what does he want?"

"Just one little thing," the wife responded. "He wants his own set of keys to the car!"

Education

124. Stephen Leacock, the Canadian professor and humorist, once wrote an anecdote about the elective system at its extreme. He had, he reported, met an American student during the summer vacation. He asked him what he was going to take in the way of courses that autumn. "Turkish, music, and architecture," the student promptly replied. "Do you expect to be choirmaster in a Turkish cathedral?" Mr. Leacock asked. "No," said the student, "those courses come at 9, 10, and 11 o'clock."

—IRWIN EDMAN

125. Once Dwight Morrow was invited to a conference of students at Amherst, and somebody put this question to him: "What course of study would you recommend for a student who plans to become a banker?"

This was his answer: "Well, I don't know that I can prescribe any special subjects that could fit him for that particular job, but I can tell you this—let him pick out from the curriculum the hardest subjects he can find, and I don't care what they are, and on top of these add the hardest one on the elective list and give to that program for the four years of his college course all the time and effort that he can muster. I won't promise you that he will become a banker, but I am sure of one thing: when he gets through, there won't be a bank in the country that won't be glad to employ him, and he may even end up becoming its president."

Efficiency

126. I am not so fond of efficiency as some are. Those energetic, neat people who go about the world furiously tidying things appall me. I like a little dirt about it. It shows that there has been activity, that people have been present, that there is life.

The neatest places I know are museums, stuffed with dead things.

—ST. JOHN ERVINE

127. Arnold Bennett had a publisher who boasted about the extraordinary efficiency of his secretary. One day while visiting the publisher's office, Bennett said to her, "Your employer claims that you're extremely efficient. What's your secret?"

"It's not my secret," the secretary replied. "It's his."

Each time she performed a service, no matter how insignificant, he never failed to acknowledge it. Because of this, she took infinite pains with her work.

Embarrassment

128. When Philip Guedalla was president of the debating society at Oxford, he begged a friend to ask him two special questions —there are always questions before the debate starts—to which he had carefully prepared answers. The friend agreed and put the first question. Mr. Guedalla's witty reply sent a ripple of laughter through the assembly. His brilliant retort to the second question brought down the house. The friend now felt it was his turn and, rising gravely from his seat once more, inquired: "What was the third question you wished me to ask you?"

Employer—Employee

129. The owner of a store was passing through the packing room and saw a boy lounging against a box and whistling cheerfully. Thinking of all his money being wasted on this type of labor, the employer asked gruffly, "How much do you get a week?"

"Ten dollars," the boy replied.

"Here's your pay for the week," said the man. "Now get out!"

On his way back to the office, the store owner ran into the foreman and asked him, "When did we hire that boy, and who is responsible for hiring him?"

"We never hired him," the foreman said. "He was just delivering a package from another firm.

—Peter Rich

130. During the noontime recreational activities the president of the corporation mounted the platform, accompanied by an overall-clad man off the assembly line, and made this speech:

"Ladies and gentlemen, you are about to see how American industry rewards those who are conscientious and hard working. This man standing beside me has been with the company less than a year,

44

during which time his unusual qualities have earned him salary increases in excess of one hundred dollars a week. I have watched him closely, observed with great pleasure the manner in which he has pitched in and gotten things done. Therefore, I am pleased to announce that starting this very afternoon he gets out of his work clothes, comes into the executive branch, and takes over an office with the title of Executive Vice President in Charge of Policy at an annual salary of $80,000. Congratulations to you, sir."

The workman shook the extended hand and said: "Gee, thanks, Dad."

Encouragement

131. A kind-hearted and sympathetic little Irish boy, walking along the street with his parish priest, was accosted by a weary organ-grinder who asked how far it was to the next town. The boy answered, "Four miles."

The priest remonstrated: "Why Michael, how can you deceive him so? You know it is eight."

"Well, your reverence," said the good-natured youngster, "I saw how tired he was, and I wanted to keep his courage up. Had I told him the truth he'd have been downhearted entirely."

Etiquette

132. "I've had a wonderful evening," said Groucho Marx to his hostess as he was leaving a dull Hollywood party, "but this wasn't it."

133. President Coolidge once invited some Vermont friends to dine at the White House. They were worried about their table manners, so decided to do everything Coolidge did. The meal passed smoothly until coffee was served and Coolidge poured his into a saucer. The guests followed suit. Then he added sugar and cream. The visitors did likewise. Then Coolidge leaned down and gave his to the cat.

—HENRY CHARLES SUTER

Exaggeration

134. A Texan was trying to impress upon a Bostonian the valor of the heroes of the Alamo. "I bet you never had anybody so brave around Boston," he said.

"Did you ever hear of Paul Revere?" asked the Bostonian.

"Paul Revere?" said the Texan. "Isn't that the guy who ran for help?"

135. When President Cleveland's second child was born, the doctor asked Cleveland to fetch a scale so that the baby's weight could be determined. Cleveland searched throughout the house without success. Finally he remembered that he had an old scale in the basement which he had used on his fishing trips. He got it and brought it upstairs. Carefully, the doctor placed the baby on the scale and was amazed to learn that the new-born infant weighed twenty-five pounds.

F

Fame

136. Jascha Heifetz and Mischa Elman were dining together when a waiter brought a letter addressed to "The Greatest Violinist in the World."

The two passed the letter back and forth, each insisting it was intended for the other. Finally they decided to open it. It began: "Dear Mr. Kreisler."

137. At a party, violinist Fritz Kreisler was entertaining his fellow guests with a dazzling display of card tricks. Later, one of the guests approached him and said:

"Would you care to perform at a party I am giving next week?"

"See my agent," said Kreisler. "He makes the financial arrangements."

The agent was consulted the next morning and the contract was signed. The following week, when Kreisler arrived at the party, he placed his violin on a chair and started to rub his hands to get the chill out of them.

His host, entering the room, took in the scene at once.

"Well," he whistled, "you play the violin, too!"

Folly

138. A very affected young man who had been holding forth at great length remarked, "I simply *can't* bear fools!"

"How odd," chimed in Dorothy Parker. "Apparently your mother could."

—OLGA SWANSON

139. Tommy's uncle was wont to give out bits of hardheaded advice to his young nephew.

"Yes, Tommy," he said one day, "fools are certain; wise men hesitate."

"Are you sure, Uncle John?" asked Tommy.

"Yes, my boy; certain of it."

Forgetfulness

140. At a big gathering in Hollywood, a celebrity seeker approached Groucho Marx with an excited "Remember me, Groucho?"

"I never forget a face," replied the funny man, "but in your case I'll make an exception."

141. Little Bobby had forgotten a schoolmate's birthday and sat down to write a note of apology.

"I have no excuse for forgetting," he wrote, "and it would serve me right if you forgot my birthday next Wednesday."

Forgiveness

142. In his autobiography Mark Twain concluded a tirade against a publisher, who had once swindled him outrageously, on a note of forgiveness.

"He has been dead a quarter of a century now," Twain wrote. "I feel only compassion for him, and if I could send him a fan I would."

143. The tennis courts of an Iowa high school adjoined the grounds of a church rectory. Occasionally, exuberant youngsters whammed a tennis ball over the fence onto the trim church lawns. One day a player, chasing a stray ball, came face to face with a large sign which read: NO TRESPASSING. The sign came down overnight, however, when the tennis club erected its own sign directly opposite. This one read: FORGIVE US OUR TRESPASSES.

Friendship

144. At a party in Hollywood, Helen Deutsch, the screen writer, noticed a new arrival antagonizing every person to whom he was intro-duced. "Young man," she told him, "you have the knack of making strangers immediately."

—Leonard Lyons

145. A visitor to the White House once asked President Lincoln, "What is your definition of a friend?"

"My definition of a friend?" the Great Emancipator repeated slowly. "One who has the same enemies you have."

—Louis Hirsch

146. Thousands of appeals for pardon came to Lincoln from soldiers involved in military discipline. Each appeal was, as a rule, supported by letters from influential people. One day a single sheet came before him, an appeal from a soldier without any supporting documents.

"What!" exclaimed the President. "Has this man no friends?"

"No, sir, not one," said the adjutant.

"Then," said Lincoln, "I will be his friend."

147. Long after graduation from Yale, Sinclair Lewis went back for a class reunion, and the banquet speakers, hailing him as the greatest of living authors, related how, even in his undergraduate days, they had recognized his genius and had been glad to help him; then, finally, he was called upon to speak, and he stood up and said something like this:

"When I came to Yale I was a freckle-faced, red-haired, gangling, gawky, greenhorn from a small town in Minnesota, and all of you either ignored me or high-hatted me. Now that I've been lucky enough to achieve a little notoriety, you've changed your tune and are trying to horn in on the act. You were not my friends then, and you're not my friends now. And as far as I'm concerned, you can all go to hell."

With that, Red Lewis walked out of the room.

Fund-Raising

148. Benjamin Franklin, who, among other things, was one of the best money raisers of his generation, once set forth his principles for the guidance of a campaign committee:

"First," he said, "call upon those who you know will give something; next apply to those of whom you are uncertain; and finally, to those you are sure will give nothing, for in some of these you may be mistaken."

149. Whenever he was asked which of his possessions he treasured most, the late Chief Justice Charles Evans Hughes, a twinkle in his eye, would lead the visitor into his study and point to a beautifully framed letter written in Spencerian script:

"In order to raise money for the church, our members are making aprons from the shirttails of famous men. We would be so pleased if you could send us one of your shirttails. Please have Mrs. Hughes mark them with your initials and also pin on them a short biography of the famous occasions in which they have been intimately associated with your life."

G

Gambling

150. Lady Godiva was the world's greatest gambler because she put everything on a horse.

151. A dining car patron on an Eastern railroad received his luncheon check, which amounted to $1.45, and gave the waiter two one-dollar bills. In due time, the waiter brought his change—a fifty-cent piece and a nickel. After a moment's hesitation, the annoyed patron picked up the half-dollar, leaving the nickel on the plate. To his surprise, the waiter grinned broadly.

"That's all right, sir," he said. "I just gambled and lost."

Genius

152. Upon finishing a highly-praised concert, Beethoven was surrounded by friends and admirers who could not say enough for his piano magic. One particularly enthusiastic woman remarked: "Oh, sir, if God had only given me that gift of genius."

Beethoven replied, "It is not genius, madam. Nor magic. All you have to do is practice on your piano eight hours a day for forty years and you'll be as good as I am."

153. A great pianist played to an audience of titled people. As he bent and swayed to his task, he rendered a delightful symphony, the like of which mortal ears are rarely privileged to hear. His performance was followed by an instant of breathless silence—then thunderous applause greeted him. It was the Queen of England who stepped forward to say, "Mr. Paderewski, you are a genius." Bowing gravely, Paderewski replied, "Before I became a genius, your Majesty, I was a drudge."

—FREDERIC W. ZIV

Gift—Gifts

154. Marc Lachman, the late publicist, used to phone bare acquaintances and ask, "What size collar do you wear?" This "hint" brought him much valuable holiday loot from people who'd planned to send him a big ten-cent greeting card, providing they couldn't get one for a nickel.

On Christmas the suckers would get plain cards from Marc saying: "To Joe, the greatest guy who ever put his head in a size 15 collar."

155. The late John M. Scribner, a prominent member of the New York bar, was bald as a bat and then some. He was speaking to

Mr. Joseph H. Choate about the approaching marriage of one of the Vanderbilts to a foreign nobleman.

"It would be absurd to give a Vanderbilt a costly gift," he said. "I should like to find something not intrinsically valuable, but interesting because it is rare."

"Nothing easier, John," Mr. Choate said. "Just send her a lock of your hair."

Giving

156. Mrs. Busybody was pumping the local lawyer about the demise of the town's richest man. "You knew him well," she cooed. "How much wealth did he leave?"

With a tip of his hat, the old lawyer replied, "All of it, madam, all of it."

157. Bessie had just received a bright new dime and was starting out to invest it in an ice cream soda.

"Why don't you give your money to the missionaries?" asked the minister who was calling at the house.

"I thought about that," said Bessie, "but I think I'll buy the ice cream soda, and let the druggist give the money to the missionaries."

158. Mark Twain used to tell the story of two women who ardently desired to see Sarah Bernhardt during her last great American tour; but after much consideration, they decided it would be sinful to spend twenty dollars—the price of two tickets—on one night's entertainment. Not to benefit by their own self-denial, they decided to give the twenty dollars to an old couple whom they knew to be in great need. And the old couple immediately went and bought two tickets to see the divine Sarah!

159. Dwight L. Moody, the great evangelist, was calling with a certain minister on a wealthy lady, to ask her help in a building operation. On the way over, Moody asked the minister what sum he had in mind. "Oh," said the pastor, "perhaps $250."

"Better let me handle the matter," suggested the evangelist.

"Madam," said Moody, after the usual introductions, "we have come to ask you for $2,000 toward the building of a new mission."

The lady threw up her hands in horror. "Oh, Mr. Moody!" she exclaimed, "I couldn't possibly give more than $1,000."

And the pair walked away with a check for just that sum.

160. One day when Horace Greeley was busy transferring his burning thoughts to paper, a representative of the Sons of Temperance succeeded in getting into the inner sanctum.

"What is it?" growled Mr. Greeley, as he continued writing. The man told his story, pleading for a contribution.

"No," glumly responded Greeley and went on with his writing. The man continued his plea and Greeley again said no. Finally the importunate one said:

"Why, Mr. Greeley, wouldn't you give me $10 to save an immortal soul from going to hell?"

"No," shouted Greeley, "not half enough people go to hell now!"

161. A minister spoke as a guest in a strange church one Sunday morning. He was accompanied by his little son.

After the worship service, the minister recalled that no offering had been taken, and as he was in the habit of never going to the Lord's house without presenting an offering, he left fifty cents in the offering box beside the door. As he and his son walked away from the church, one of the church officers came running after them, saying, "It is our custom here to give to the preacher whatever we find in the offering box after the service." And the man handed to the minister the coin he himself had left there.

Whereupon the little boy looked up into his father's face and observed, "Papa, if you had given more, you would have gotten more, wouldn't you?"

162. A witty person once said: "There are three kinds of givers in the world—the flint, the sponge, and the honeycomb."

To get anything out of a flint, you must hammer it, and then you get only flint and sparks.

To get anything out of a sponge you must squeeze, and the more you squeeze the sponge, the more you will get.

But the honeycomb overflows with its own sweetness.

Some people are stingy and hard; they give nothing away if they can help it.

Others are good natured; they yield to pressure, and the more they are pressed, the more readily and abundantly they give.

A few delight in giving without being asked at all, and of these, the *Bible* says: "The Lord loveth a cheerful giver."

God—Man

163. Henry Ford was asked one day if he ever worried, and he replied, "No, I believe God is managing affairs and that He doesn't need any advice from me. With God in charge, I believe that everything will work out for the best in the end. So what is there to worry about?"

164. Once when Lord Moynihan, great British surgeon, had finished operating before a gallery full of distinguished visiting doctors, he was asked how he could work with such a crowd present. He replied: "You see there are just three people in the operating room when I operate—the patient and myself." "But that is only two!" his questioner commented. "Who is the third?" Moynihan responded, "The third is God."

Golden Rule

165. A six-year-old and her four-year-old brother had a difference of opinion which finally led to blows.

"Children! Children!" exclaimed their mother. "Haven't you heard of the Golden Rule?"

"Yes," sputtered the six-year-old, "but he did unto me first."

166. A mother happening one day to overhear a group of little girls excitedly concocting a scheme of revenge against another little girl, who apparently had done something very "mean," was grieved to find her own child among the chief conspirators.

"Why, my dear!" she said, taking her child aside, "it seems to me you're going to do to Lottie just what you don't want her to do to you. I don't think this is the Golden Rule—is it?"

"Well, mama," said the child, "the Golden Rule is all right for Sunday, but for everyday I'd rather have an eye for an eye and a tooth for a tooth!"

Gossip

167. Gossip was distasteful to Mrs. Hannah More, the English writer. Whenever a visitor or friend brought up any gossip, Mrs. More would say, "Come, we will go and ask if this is true."

The talebearer was always so taken aback that she would beg to be excused. But the determined Mrs. More insisted on escorting the gossiper to the one of whom the story was told.

No one ever repeated the offense in Mrs. More's presence after that.

168. An old man invested in one of those new hearing aids that are practically invisible, and he was assured by the salesman that he could return it if it didn't prove twice as effective as the cumbersome device he had been using for a number of years. He returned in a few days to express his great satisfaction with the new device.

"I'll bet your family likes it too," hazarded the clerk. "Oh, they don't even know I've got it," chuckled the old gent. "And do you know what, I'm having a perfectly grand time with it! Just in the past two days I've changed my will twice!"

Grandparent—Grandparents

169. A grandmother recently met her friend and started to ask, "Did I tell you about the cute thing my granddaughter said . . ."

But she was cut short with, "Before you start I warn you that I demand equal time—and I have sixteen grandchildren!"

170. "Little did I realize when we stood before the minister," said the silver-haired father, "that forty years later, and without any teeth, I'd be eating peanut brittle to keep from hurting the feelings of a twelve-year-old granddaughter whose Scout troop is selling the stuff."

171. There was a grandmother who was so tickled to learn that her grandchildren were coming for a week that she put a five-dollar bill in the collection plate at church. When they went home at the end of the week, her joy must have been double because that Sunday she put a ten-dollar bill in the plate.

Gratitude

172. A little girl approached a great concert violinist after his performance and asked him for his autograph. "I'm sorry," said the maestro, "but my hands are so very tired from playing."

"My hands are tired, too," said the little girl, "and they're tired from applauding."

173. The priest was trying to comfort one of his parishioners. "Mr. Kelly," he said, "you shouldn't be bitter. You must be thankful." "Thankful!" exclaimed Kelly. "Just what have I to be thankful for, I ask you? I can't even pay my bills."

The priest thought for a bit, then said brightly: "Why, man alive, be thankful you aren't one of your creditors."

174. A traveler in Europe was overcome with cold and fatigue and was about to compose himself in what he expected to be a sleep of death when a truck driver came by and rescued him. The rescued man wanted to pay him, but the driver considered it an insult to be paid for what he counted a common duty—to help a fellow man in distress.

"At least," the traveler said, "tell me your name so I can have you in thankful remembrance before God."

"Are you a Christian?" the truck driver asked.

Learning that he was, the driver asked, "Can you tell me the name of the Good Samaritan?" Of course the Christian traveler could not.

"Then," said the truck driver, "neither will I tell you mine."

H

Habit—Habits

175. An old story tells of a father who, in guiding his son, told him to drive a nail into a post every time he did an evil thing, and to withdraw one nail each time he did a good act. The son did so, but regretted he could not pull out the nail holes. So with the record of every life. We may amend, change our program, turn over a new leaf— but some flaws remain. Habits long continued become hard to break. The nail holes stay, and they remind us of bad decisions.

176. A young fellow who was an inveterate cigarette smoker went to the country for a vacation. Reaching the small town in the early morning, he wanted a smoke, but there was no store open. He saw a boy smoking a cigarette, and approached him, saying:

"Say, my boy, have you got another cigarette?"

"No, sir," said the boy, "but I've got the makings."

"All right," the city chap said. "But I can't roll 'em very well. Will you fix one for me?"

"Sure," said the boy.

"Don't believe I've got a match," said the man, as he searched his pockets.

The boy handed him a match.

"Say," the boy said, "you ain't got anything but the habit, have you?"

Handwriting

177. The physician had been sent an invitation to dinner. In reply, the hostess received an absolutely illegible note. "I've got to know if he accepts or refuses," she told a friend, "but I simply can't read this note."

"Take it to a druggist," the friend advised. "No matter how badly written, a druggist can always read a doctor's handwriting."

The druggist looked at the slip of paper, disappeared into a back room and returned in a few minutes with a small bottle. "Here you are," he said, "that will be one seventy-five."

Happiness

178. Some of our foremost successful men, Edison, Ford, Belasco, Roosevelt, and Carnegie, have told how happy they were in their work, and how their success was the result of the love they put into it. Neither money, fame, nor luxury was the goal of these men; these are merely the things which are added to those who succeed in

doing their work well. The richest men and the greatest artists all
testify that it is the work itself which constitutes happiness.

—RICHARD LYNCH

179. In the cornerstone for its new office building in Minneapolis,
the Prudential Life Insurance Company placed predictions by twenty
leading citizens as to what life in the United States will be like in the
year 1975.

Among the forecasts was one from Harry Bullis, chairman of General
Mills. First he gave some eye-opening estimates of increased popula-
tion, wealth, income and living standards. These he topped off with this
wise and wonderful reminder:

"In 1975, men and women will still struggle for happiness—*which
will continue to lie within themselves.*"

Hatred

180. Charles Lamb once said: "Don't introduce me to that man!
I want to go on hating him, and I can't hate a man whom I know."

181. Booker T. Washington, the great Negro educator, was walking down a street with a white friend when he was roughly elbowed
into the gutter by a passing pedestrian. His friend was furious, exclaim-
ing, "How can you tolerate such an insult?" To which Washington replied, "I defy any man to make me hate."

—JAY SABO

Health

182. The human body is wonderfully strong. Even when it is
defective it will go on for thirty or forty years. The late John D. Rocke-
feller had gastritis and nervous dyspepsia at forty, but he lived to be

nearly ninety-eight. Cecil Rhodes had lung trouble at twenty-one. A doctor told him he had only six months to live. But he lived to be forty-nine. Herbert Spencer was an invalid all his life, but he wielded a world-wide influence and lived to be eighty-three.

Helpfulness

183. A mother had been lecturing her small son, stressing that we are in this world to help others. He considered this for some time, then asked somberly: "What are the others here for?"

184. Julia Ward Howe one day was talking to Charles Sumner, the distinguished senator from Massachusetts. She asked him to interest himself in the case of a person who needed some help. The senator answered, "Julia, I've become so busy I can no longer concern myself with individuals." Julia replied, "Charles, that is quite remarkable. Even God hasn't reached that stage yet."

—Ralph W. Sockman

History

185. When the famed historian, Charles A. Beard, was asked if he could summarize the great lessons of history, he replied in four short sentences: 1. Whom the gods would destroy, they first make mad with power. 2. The mills of the gods grind slowly, but they grind exceedingly fine. 3. The bee fertilizes the flower it robs. 4. When it is dark enough, you can see the stars.

186. Once a week a ninety-year-old grandmother walks the six blocks from her house to the village library. Recently she made her book selection and appeared at the desk with a racy best-seller.

"Why, I thought you never read anything but history," the young librarian said, plainly shocked by this prim little person.

The grandmother's cheeks turned pink, but she tucked the book into her knitting bag defiantly. "My dear," she replied, "at my age THIS is history."

Husband—Wife

187. A tired businessman's grueling day at the office was capped by his wife's announcement that the cook had walked out.

"Again?" moaned the husband. "What was the trouble this time?"

"You were!" charged the wife. "She said you used insulting language to her over the phone this morning."

"Good grief!" confessed the husband. "I thought all the time I was talking to *you*."

188. "I'm the head of my house," remarked one recently-wed husband to another. "I should be, after all I'm the one who earns the money."

"Well," said the other, "my wife and I have a different arrangement. We've agreed that I should decide all the major problems and she the minor ones."

"How is that working out?" asked the first.

"All I can report is that so far no problems of major importance have come up."

189. Paderewski, the great Polish pianist, was seated next to Mrs. Dwight W. Morrow at a dinner. She was the wife of the ambassador to Mexico in the Coolidge administration. In the course of their conversation she told him how she enjoyed his concerts when a girl in school. He asked if she enjoyed going back to visit her alma mater. She replied that she did, and when back at school couldn't help thinking how much the happiness in her life had exceeded her fondest expectations.

"You mean you are happier now than you at eighteen expected you would be?" Paderewski asked, keenly interested.

"Yes, indeed!" Mrs. Morrow answered.

"Mrs. Morrow," said Paderewski, with an old-world bow, "I would like to meet your husband."

I

Identification

190. A haughty dowager visited the hospital to see her chauffeur, who had been badly injured in an automobile accident. The head nurse hesitated, then said: "He's a very sick man and should see no one but members of his family. Are you his wife?"

Highly indignant, the dowager blurted out: "I certainly am not; I'm his mistress."

191. On a visit to the White House, ventriloquist Edgar Bergen was stopped at the gate by Secret Service men and asked to show identification. Fumbling through his pockets, Edgar could find nothing that satisfied the guards. At last he said, "All I've got is Charlie Mc-Carthy here." He opened the grip that held Charlie. The dummy sat up, nodded and said, "Yeah, fellows, he's Edgar Bergen."

Without further fuss, the Secret Service men gestured Edgar into the White House.

192. When the great Charles Darwin was visiting the country house of a friend, the two boys of the family thought they would play a trick on the scientist. They caught a butterfly, a grasshopper, a beetle, and a centipede, and out of these evolved a strange composite insect. They took the centipede's body, the butterfly's wings, the grass-hopper's legs, and the beetle's head, glued them carefully together and presented it to Darwin for identification. Darwin looked at the bug and then at the boys.

"Did you notice whether it made a humming sound when you caught it, boys?" he asked.

"Yes," they answered.

"Then," said Darwin, with a twinkle in his eye, "it's a hum-bug."

Illustration—Illustrations

193. Once, when Toscanini was rehearsing Debussy's *La Mer*, he wanted to achieve a highly evanescent effect in one spot. At a loss for words to describe what he wanted, he took from his breastpocket a large, white silk handkerchief. He threw it high into the air, and every man in the orchestra was hypnotized as it floated softly, sensuously, to the floor. "There," the maestro smiled happily, "play it like that."

194. The man was charged with assault and battery. Throughout the cross-examination he maintained he had merely pushed his victim "a little bit."

"Well, about how hard?" asked prosecuting counsel.

"Oh, just a little bit."

"Now," said counsel, "for the benefit of the judge and jury, you will please step down here and, with me for a subject, illustrate just how hard you mean."

The defendant descended and approached the waiting counsel. When he reached him the spectators were amazed to see him slap the lawyer in the face, seize him bodily, and finally, with a supreme effort, lift him from the floor and hurl him prostrate across the table.

Turning from the bewildered counsel, he faced the Court and explained, mildly, "Your lordship and gentlemen, about one-tenth that hard!"

Ingenuity. See also Resourcefulness

195. In a crowded hall a little Irishman rose to his feet and asked in stentorian tones: "Is there a Christian Scientist in the hall?"

Receiving no answer he repeated his question, and in the opposite corner a little, poetical looking fellow stood and said: "I am a Christian Scientist."

"Then would ye mind changin' seats with me, there's a draft here on my back."

—MORRIS FISHBEIN

196. In a volume of reminiscences, Sir Henry Luey related the following story: One of Queen Victoria's grandsons wrote to her for a "tip." She replied, "warning the youth against the consequences of forming extravagant habits in early youth," whereupon he replied: "Dearest Grandma—I received your letter and hope you do not think that I was disappointed because you could not send me the money. It was very kind of you to give me the good advice, and I sold your letter for forty pounds, ten shillings."

Inspiration

197. A great musician one day visited the celebrated painter Matisse at his home on the shores of the Mediterranean. He asked Matisse, "What is your inspiration?"

"I grow artichokes," replied Matisse. "Every morning I go into the garden and watch these plants. I see the play of light and shade on the leaves and I discover new combinations of colors and fantastic patterns. They inspire me. Then I go back into the studio and paint."

Surely, if artichokes can provide inspiration for a great artist, the common things of life we so often overlook must hold much of inspiration for us.

—JOHN H. CROWE

198. Bruce Barton once gave a talk before an evening class in writing. One of the students asked, "Mr. Barton, where do you get the inspiration for your magazine articles?"

"Well," said Mr. Barton, "picture me sitting at breakfast in the morning. As I sip my coffee, my wife across the table glances down at the floor and observes, 'Bruce, we really need a new dining room rug. This one is wearing through.' Right there I have the inspiration to write another article."

The students were disappointed in this answer, little realizing they had been let in on the great secret of inspiration in nearly every field of human activity—*necessity.*

Insurance

199. A 97-year-old man presented himself at the insurance office and said he wished to take out a policy on his life. He filled in an application blank but was very much annoyed when he was turned down.

"You folks are making a big mistake," he said, "if you look over your statistics you'll discover that mighty few men die after they're 97."

200. The insistent salesman had his prospect backed against the wall. "Take our accident insurance policy," he insisted.

The prospect still had some fight left. "Why should I?" he asked defensively.

"Listen!" boasted the salesman. "One month ago a man took out a policy with us. The other day he broke his neck and we paid him $5,000. Now think: tomorrow you may be the lucky one!"

Integrity

201. One of two women riding on a bus suddenly realized she hadn't paid her fare. "I'll go right up and pay it," she declared.

"Why bother?" her friend replied. "You got away with it—so what?"

"I've found that honesty always pays," the other said virtuously, and went up to pay the driver.

"See, I told you honesty pays!" she said when she returned. "I handed the driver a quarter and he gave me change for fifty cents."

202. Two piles of apples lay on the ground. One contained a large-sized and rosy selection; the fruit of the other was green and small.

"Large on the top, sir, and small at the bottom?" inquired the new packing clerk, as he prepared to fill a barrel.

"Certainly not!" replied the farmer. "Honesty is the best policy, my boy. Put the little apples at the top, and the large ones at the bottom."

The boy complied. "Is the barrel full, my lad?" asked the farmer.

"Yes," replied the boy.

"Good," said the farmer. "Now turn it upside down and label it."

Interference

203. "Everyone in town is talking about the Smith quarrel," remarked the wife. "Some are taking his part and some are taking hers . . ."

"And," interrupted her husband, "I suppose a few eccentric individuals are minding their own business."

204. After an active life as scientist and statesman, the late Chaim Weizmann could not reconcile himself to the office of first President of Israel. His duties were severely limited in scope and nature under Israel legislation, and Dr. Weizmann, accustomed to a busy political life, found little to occupy his time.

Once, while reviewing an Israeli army parade, he dropped his handkerchief. A brigadier general sitting nearby returned it to him. The President thanked the general effusively and went on in the same strain for several minutes.

The general, bewildered at this display of gratitude, said, "But all I did was to return your handkerchief, sir."

"Yes, but you don't understand how valuable it is to me," the President rejoined gravely, but with a twinkle in his eye. "You see, it's all that's left for me to stick my nose into these days."

—JULIAN MELTZER

Intolerance

205. When you hear a man say, "I hate," adding the name of some race, nation, religion, or social class, you are dealing with a belated mind. That man may dress like a modern, ride in an automobile, listen over the radio, but his mind is properly dated about 1000 B.C.

—HARRY EMERSON FOSDICK

206. A friend got tired of hearing a certain man say, "Isn't that just like a Jew?" The next time he raised the question, my friend replied with another: "Which Jew do you mean, Shylock or Christ?" Try it some time yourself and see how it sharpens the focus. The next time somebody says to you, "Isn't that just like a Negro?" you ask, "Which Negro do you mean, Old Black Joe or George Washington Carver? Little Black Sambo or Marian Anderson?"

—ROBERT W. MOORE

Intoxication. See also Alcoholic Liquor

207. A fellow we know who goes to work at 6:30 every morning told us that as he left home one day recently he saw a neighbor fumbling drunkenly with the key to his front door. The police officer on the beat came to his aid and asked jokingly, "Where are you going at this hour?"

"To a lecture," replied the drunk.

208. One day, so an Arab legend goes, the Devil presented himself to a man and said, "You are about to die. I can save you from death under any one of three ways—kill your servant, or beat your wife, or drink this wine."

"Let me think," said the man. "To kill my faithful servant is impossible; to mistreat my wife is ridiculous. I will drink the wine."

He drank the wine, and being drunk, he beat his wife and killed his servant who attempted to defend her.

209. There is a story told of a somewhat tipsy man who piled into a crowded bus, and lurched into a seat beside a priest. He sat for a few minutes, blearily eyeing the priest, who was reading his Office. Then suddenly he said in a loud voice, "I ain't going to heaven, because I feel there ain't no heaven!" The priest, pretending not to hear, buried his nose in his breviary. At this the man bellowed at the top of his lungs: "I said, I ain't going to heaven, because there ain't no heaven! Now what do you say, padre?" The priest replied: "Well, go to hell then, but do be quiet about it!"

—CLARE BOOTHE LUCE

Invention—Inventions

210. Before the turn of the century, a bishop, paying his annual visit to a small religious college, was discussing the state of the world while a guest at the home of one of the professors. He ventured the opinion that because everything about nature had been discovered and inasmuch as all possible inventions had been made, the world was on the verge of the millennium. The professor disagreed. He said the next fifty years would produce many discoveries. "Many!" cried the bishop, "name one." The professor replied that in the next few years man would be able to fly like the birds. "Nonsense," exclaimed the bishop. "Flight is reserved for the angels."

The bishop's name was WRIGHT—he had two sons, Orville and Wilbur.

211. One afternoon Mark Twain, who lost more than one hard-earned fortune by investing it in harebrained schemes described to him in glittering terms, observed a tall, spare man with kindly blue eyes and eager face, coming up the path with a strange contraption under his arm. Yes, it was an invention, and the man explained it to the humorist, who listened politely but said he had been burned too often.

"But I'm not asking you **to** invest a fortune," explained the man. "You can have as large a share as you want for $500." Mark Twain shook his head; the invention didn't make sense. The tall, stooped figure started away.

"What did you say your name was?" the author called after him.

"Bell," replied the inventor a little sadly, "Alexander Graham Bell."

—VANSANT CORYELL

J

Joint Effort

212. A visitor to a mental hospital was astonished to note that watching over a hundred dangerous inmates were only three guards. He asked, "Don't you feel these people will overpower the guards and escape?" He got the reply, "No, lunatics never unite."

213. Two moving men were struggling with a big crate in a doorway. They pushed and tugged until they were exhausted but it wouldn't move. Finally, the man on the outside said, "We'd better give up, we'll never get this in."

The fellow on the inside said, "What do you mean get it in, I thought you were trying to get it out."

Journalism. See also Newspaper

214. "Remember," said the editor to a young lady reporter, "it was Joseph Pulitzer, the great newspaperman, who declared that accuracy is to a newspaper what virtue is to a woman."

"That, in itself, is not entirely accurate," said the young miss triumphantly. "A newspaper can always print a retraction."

215. A British fledgling reporter had been reprimanded for his overlong accounts and told to be brief. His next story was turned in as follows: "A shocking incident occurred last night. Sir Reggy Blank, a guest at Lady Briny's ball, complained of feeling ill, took his hat, his coat, his departure, no notice of his friends, a taxi, a pistol from his pocket and finally, his life. Nice chap. Regrets and all that."

Justice

216. They had been married just two weeks and he was going through a batch of mail. "Honey," he said, "aren't these bills for the clothes you bought before we were married?"

"Yes, darling," she replied. "You're not upset about it, are you?"

"Well," he retorted, "don't you think it's unfair to ask a fish to pay for the bait he was caught with?"

217. Two police magistrates were driving home together at night, when they were stopped by a motorcycle policeman. They were duly charged and, when their cases came up for hearing the next day, they agreed that each should leave the bench in turn to have his case heard by the other.

The first went to trial, pleaded guilty and was find $10 and costs. When they changed places the second magistrate, after pleading guilty, was shocked to receive a fine of $15 and costs. "That's a bit unfair," he complained. "I fined you only $10."

"I know," was the reply, "but there is too much of this sort of thing going on—this is the second case we've had today."

K

Know-How

218. A New York socialite came into the salon of Walter Florell, mad milliner to movie stars and society, and announced she needed a hat at once for a cocktail party. Walter took a couple of yards of ribbon, twisted it around, put it on her head and said, "There is your hat, madam." The lady looked in the mirror and exclaimed, "It's wonderful."

"Twenty-five dollars," said Walter.

"But that's too much for a couple of yards of ribbon!"

Florell unwound the ribbon and handed it to her saying, "The ribbon, madam, is free."

—ERSKINE JOHNSON

219. Two farmers at a county fair were fascinated by a booth where little celluloid balls bobbed on top of water jets. Customers were offered substantial prizes if they succeeded in shooting any one of the balls off its perch. One of the farmers spent six quarters in a vain effort to pick off one ball. Finally his friend pushed him aside and picked up the rifle.

"Watch how I do it," he said. He took a single shot. All six balls disappeared.

As they walked away from the booth, laden with prizes, the unsuccessful one marveled. "How did you ever do it?" he asked.

"It just took knowing how," explained the winner. "I shot the man working the pump."

Knowledge

220. Most men believe it would benefit them if they could get a little from those who *have* more. How much more would it benefit them if they would learn a little from those who *know* more.

—WILLIAMS J. H. BOETCKER

L

Law

221. "One of the finest examples of the value of precedent that I have ever seen," President James Burrill Angell, of the University of Michigan, used to say to his class in International Law, "is one of the paths which you fellows make across the grass of the campus. We take that as clear proof that a walk should be there, and set about building one."

222. The famous Rufus Choate, than whom there was never a shrewder cross-examiner, was questioning a witness in an assault case in which his client was the accused. He maneuvered the fellow into admitting that he hadn't actually seen the offense committed.

"So," purred the famous attorney, "you say you didn't actually see the defendant bite off this man's ear?"

"Naw," growled the witness, "I didn't see him bite it off. I just seen him spit it out on the ground!"

The jury roared—and Choate knew full well he had lost his case on that one break.

—PAUL W. KEARNEY

223. *Courtroom strategy:* A. S. Trude, the famed trial lawyer, and the distinguished Dr. Frank Billings lived next door to each other in Chicago. One day Billings testified as a medical expert against Trude. Trude's cross-examination of his eminent neighbor was brief. "Was Marshall Field one of your patients?" he began.

"Yes."

Trude asked, "Where is Mr. Field now?" and the Doctor said, "Dead." Trude named other patients of Billings—Mr. Armour, Mr. Pullman, Mr. Cudahy, all of whom had died natural deaths. Each time Trude asked: "Where is he now?" and each time Dr. Billings had to answer: "Dead."

"That's all, thank you," the lawyer concluded, and won his case.

—LEONARD LYONS

Lawyer—Lawyers

224. Returning from a visit to his birthplace, Clarence Darrow, the noted criminal lawyer, met a doctor friend. "If you had listened to me," said the friend, "you, too, would be a doctor."

"Why, what's the matter with being a lawyer?"

"I don't say that all lawyers are crooks," said the doctor, "but even you will have to admit that your profession doesn't exactly make angels of men."

"No," replied Darrow, "you doctors have the better of us there."

225. George Ade had finished his after-dinner speech, and when he had seated himself a well-known lawyer, also an amateur wit, rose, shoved his hands deep into his trouser pockets, as was his habit, and laughingly inquired: "Doesn't it strike the company as a little unusual that a professional humorist should be funny?"

When the laughter had subsided, Ade drawled: "Doesn't it strike the company as a little unusual that a lawyer should have his hands in his own pockets?"

Laziness

226. Abraham Lincoln once took a sack of grain to a mill whose proprietor was known to be the laziest man in Illinois. After watching the miller for a while, the future president commented wearily, "I can eat that grain as fast as you're grinding it."

"Indeed," grunted the miller, "and how long do you think you could keep that up?"

"Until I starve to death," replied Lincoln.

227. An Eastern go-getter spied a lazy Indian chief lolling at the door of his tepee somewhere out West. "Chief," remonstrated the go-getter, "why don't you get yourself a job?"

"Why?" grunted the chief.

"You could earn money. Maybe fifty or sixty dollars a week."

"Why?" insisted the chief.

"Oh, if you worked hard and saved your money, you'd soon have a bank account. Wouldn't you like that?"

"Why?" again asked the chief.

"For gosh sakes!" shouted the exasperated go-getter. "With a big bank account you could retire, and then you wouldn't have to work anymore—"

"I'm not working now," pointed out the Indian.

Little Things

228. An old gardener while laying a stone wall in a country estate was asked by the owner why he used so many small stones along with the large ones. "It's like this," he said, "these stones are like men. Many small men like me are needed to keep the big ones in place. If I leave small stones out, the big ones will not stay in place and the wall will fall."

—S. Kenrick Guernsey

Luck

229. David, a second-grader, was bumped while getting on the school bus and suffered a two-inch cut on his cheek. At recess he collided with another boy and two of his teeth were knocked loose. At noon while sliding on ice, he fell and broke his wrist. Later at the hospital, his father noticed David clutching a quarter in his good hand. "I found it on the ground when I fell," David said. "This is the first quarter I ever found. This sure is my lucky day."

230. Once when Governor Mennen Williams of Michigan visited one of the large automobile manufacturing plants in Detroit, an entire auto was assembled in his honor in the record time of ten minutes. The event was recorded in the daily press on a wide scale from one end of the country to the other. Shortly thereafter an official of the company received a long-distance call from an aroused citizen. "I read in the papers where you put together an automobile in ten minutes one day last month, is that true?"

"Yes, it is and it was done in the presence of the Governor," was the reply.

"Well, I don't care for whom it was done. It was my bad luck to get it and I demand that you replace it with another."

M

Man—Woman

231. Two old-timers were standing on a street corner discussing the ills of the world. "Our whole trouble started," one of them said, "when women began to take over men's work. Women work in the factory, filling station, markets, and . . ."

Just then two girls who had been away at different colleges met near where the old men were standing. They grabbed each other in a bear hug and danced in delight.

The men looked on silently; then the old-timer who had been interrupted by the display of affection, said, "Just like I told you. Women are doing men's work."

—BURTON A. MILEY

232. Sixty-five percent of women say they'd rather be men. Men do have more freedom. But beyond that—well, the modern gal certainly can't complain.

A married woman has her bills paid the rest of her life. She has to keep house—but she never catches the really tough jobs.

She doesn't have to be a coal miner, fire fighter, slaughterhouse worker, blast furnace worker, garbage collector, steel worker, seaman, or any of a hundred others. Women collect 80% of all life insurance, 63% of all inheritances. They own between 55% and 60% of all savings accounts. They live five years longer than men, are less likely to wind up in jail or insane asylums or in debt. A male is four times more likely to be killed by someone else. Law courts are more lenient toward women.

Besides, women can marry men. In 1700, Mary Montagu said, "It goes far toward reconciling me to being a woman when I reflect I am in no danger of marrying one."

—ERNEST E. BLAU

Marriage

233. Running into her former suitor at a party, a girl decided to snub him.

"So sorry," she murmured when the hostess introduced him, "but I didn't get the name."

"I know you didn't," said the unabashed ex-suitor, "but you certainly tried hard enough."

234.   An English soldier in a French village, seeing a wedding in process at a church, asked a Frenchman whose wedding it was.

"*Je ne sais pas, M'sieu*," answered the Frenchman.

A few hours later the same soldier saw a coffin going into the same church, and curiosity getting the better of him, he again asked the identity of the individual.

"*Je ne sais pas*," was the response.

"Blimey!" ejaculated the Tommy, "he didn't last long."

235.   M. le Vicomte Sorigny, a distinguished member of the French Embassy, was present at the silver wedding anniversary celebration of a bishop. Leaning over to his neighbor, the bishop's nephew, the Vicomte asked, *sotto voce:* "Tell me, what is this silver wedding which we celebrate? I do not quite understand."

"Oh," replied the bishop's nephew, "don't you know? My uncle and aunt have lived together for 25 years without ever having been separated."

"Ah," exclaimed the diplomat heartily, "and now he marry her? Br-ravo!"

Mental Illness

236.   A vacationer at a summer resort, which was located near a state mental hospital, stopped during a walk to watch one of the inmates "painting" the fence with a dry brush and an empty bucket.

"I don't really belong here," the patient confided, "but my people say I believe anything anyone tells me and do crazy things. They say I took $10,000 out of my savings account when someone told me the banks aren't safe, and I don't know where I hid it."

"Really," said the vacationer, his eyes brightening.

"Oh, I know all right," protested the patient. He pointed to a big sycamore in the woods adjacent to the institution. "I buried it under that tree until I get out of here."

Early the next morning the vacationer was back to see the inmate, who was again "painting" the fence. The vacationer looked exhausted and sleepy.

"Say," he asked petulantly, "are you sure it was under that big sycamore where you buried your $10,000?"

The patient gleefully looked him over from head to foot and then laughed heartily. "Get yourself a brush and bucket, pal," he said. "You're just like me."

Mistake—Mistakes

237. At the end of the day, one of the bank officers was closing the door when he noticed a customer outside with bundles in his arms and a perplexed look on his face, staring at the night depository. The officer approached him and asked if he could help.

The man replied excitedly: "My wife will shoot me!"

"What happened?"

"I dropped the wrong package down the chute."

"What was in it?"

"Pork chops."

—E. E. Snyder

238. Many of the world's finest oriental rugs come from little villages in the Middle East. Each rug is hand-produced by a crew of men and boys under the direction of a master weaver. Since ordinarily they work from the under side of the rug-to-be, it frequently happens that a weaver absent-mindedly makes a mistake and introduces a color that is not according to the pattern. When this occurs, the master weaver, instead of having the work pulled out in order to correct the color sequence, will find some way to incorporate the mistake harmoniously into the overall pattern. . . . It is a useful object lesson, for we all can learn to take unexpected difficulties and mistakes and weave them advantageously into the greater pattern of our lives.

There is an inherent good in most difficulties.

—Norman Vincent Peale

Misunderstanding

239. At Arthur Murray's dance studio, an over-anxious pupil frequently danced the steps without waiting for her tutor's lead. Finally he said, "Pardon me, but aren't you anticipating?"

"Why, Mr. Fowler," she said blushing furiously, "I'm not even married."

240. President Taft had a reception at the White House which was attended by Government officials, members of the Army and Navy, members of the diplomatic corps, and leading Washington citizens. As these lined up to shake hands with the President, the President's tailor also fell into line. As he reached Taft, the latter grasped his hand, remarking, "You look familiar to me, but I just can't place you." "Why, Mr. President," the tailor replied, "I made your pants." "Oh, yes, yes, why how do you do Major Pants," was the President's reply.

241. Mr. Ginsburg, en route to Europe, was assigned by the head steward to a table for two. Presently he was joined by a polite Frenchman who, before sitting down, bowed, smiled, and said, "*Bon appetit.*" Not to be outdone, Mr. Ginsburg rose, bowed, and said, "Ginsburg."

This little ceremony was repeated at each meal for three days. The Frenchman always came late, always said, "*Bon appetit,*" and his bewildered table companion always rose and replied, "Ginsburg."

On the fourth day, Mr. Ginsburg confided his perplexity to a man in the smoking lounge: "This Frenchman tells me his name—Bon Appetit —and then I tell him mine. So we are introduced. That's fine. But why keep it up day after day, meal after meal?"

"Oh, but you don't understand, Mr. Ginsburg," replied the other. *Bon appetit* is not his name. He is merely wishing you a good appetite, he is hoping that you have a pleasant meal."

"Ah, now I understand," exclaimed Ginsburg. "Thanks for helping me out. Now I'll have to show him that I know what he means."

That evening it was Ginsburg who arrived late for dinner. Before sitting down he bowed ceremoniously, and said, *"Bon appetit."*

Whereupon the Frenchman rose, smiled, and murmured, "Ginsburg."

Music Appreciation

242. Jascha Heifetz gave a violin concert in Boston during the dead of winter. It was a miserable night, with snow, sleet, and hail. As a result, the big concert hall, which normally seats 2,500 people, had twelve in the audience. Heifetz came out on stage and said, "I'm deeply appreciative that you folks turned out, but under the circumstances, we're canceling the show. Your money will be refunded at the box office."

Eleven of the twelve started to get their money. The lone man stood and said, "Just a minute, Mr. Heifetz, I'm a music lover. I drove twenty miles through this snow. I even put chains on my car to come here and see you tonight. Won't you sing just one song?"

N

Name—Names

243. Many years ago the Brown Hotel in Louisville, Kentucky, adopted the custom of naming a room in the hotel for each winner of the Kentucky Derby. There was a Zev Room, a Gallant Fox Room, a Whirlaway Room, etc. But after the 1946 Derby, the management decided to abandon the practice. The winner that year was Assault.

244. R. B. Jones doesn't have a first or middle name, only the initials, which never were a problem until R. B. went to work for a

U.S. Government agency. The Government is not accustomed to initialed but nameless employees, but R. B. finally was given official forms to fill in for the payroll and personnel departments, and his name was entered as R (only) B (only) Jones.

Sure enough, when R. B. got his pay check, it was made out to Ronly Bonly Jones.

245. Nicholas Longworth, better known as "Nick," was a popular speaker of the House of Representatives. It had been said of him while he lived that "If Nick Longworth were to die today, more cheeks would be wet with physical tears than for any other man in public life in Washington." Longworth came from a most distinguished family of Cincinnati. There is a story told of his great-grandfather, who, calling on Longfellow, remarked that his name and the poet's began with the same syllable. Longfellow answered, "You have the better of the argument. Worth makes the man, and want of it the fellow."

Neighbor—Neighbors

246. A woman in the suburbs was chatting over the back fence with her next-door neighbor. "We're going to be living in a better neighborhood soon," she said.

"So are we," her neighbor volunteered.

"What? Are you moving, too?"

"No, we're staying here."

247. One day the richest woman in town went to visit an old woman living in a tenement, and in great need. There was no food in the dingy kitchen; no money for rent. "I'll see that a settlement worker visits you in the morning," said the grand dame, as she planned a hasty exit.

The old woman proudly replied: "You needn't trouble yourself; I need no help."

At that moment another woman, from upstairs in the tenement, entered with food and clothing. She was warmly welcomed. When the rich visitor asked for an explanation, the tenement-dweller replied, "You see, she's a *neighbor*."

Newspaper—Newspapers. See also Journalism

248. Walter Winchell's favorite story, which may be apocryphal, is about an editorial feud between the old *New York Sun* and the *New York Post,* when both were conservative papers. One day the very proper and staid *Post* lost its temper and editorially called the *Sun* a yellow dog. The Sun replied in its starchiest manner:

"The *Post* calls the *Sun* a yellow dog. The attitude of the *Sun,* however, will continue to be that of any dog toward any post."

249. Mark Twain, in his reporting days, was instructed by an editor never to state anything as a fact that he could not verify from personal knowledge. Sent to cover an important social event soon afterward, he turned in the following story:

"A woman giving the name of Mrs. James Jones, who is reported to be one of the society leaders of the city, is said to have given what purported to be a party yesterday to a number of alleged ladies. The hostess claims to be the wife of a reputed attorney."

O

Obstacle—Obstacles

250. A biologist tells how he watched an ant carrying a piece of straw which seemed a big burden for it. The ant came to a crack in the earth which was too wide for it to cross. It stood for a time as though pondering the situation, then put the straw across the crack and walked over upon it.

Here is a lesson for all mankind! A man's burden can be made a bridge for his progress.

251. John Wesley was walking one day with a man who expressed his doubt of God's goodness. "I don't know what I shall do with all my worries and troubles," he said.

At that moment Wesley noticed a cow looking over a stone wall. "Do you know," asked Wesley, "why that cow is looking over the wall?"

"No," replied his troubled companion.

"I will tell you," said Wesley. "Because she can't see through it. That is what you must do with your wall of trouble—look over it and above it."

Old Age

252. A reporter asked the late Lionel Barrymore, toward the end of his life, if he still found acting as much fun as it used to be.

"Look, son, I'm 75 years old," Barrymore snorted. "Nothing is as much fun as it used to be."

253. On the occasion of his 100th birthday, a man was being interviewed by a reporter. He answered promptly all the questions put to him until the reporter asked him to what he attributed the fact that he'd reached such a milestone.

There was a rather long pause, and then the old man drawled, "Well, I guess the main reason I got to be 100 years old is that I was born in 1865."

254. When Sarah Bernhardt, the celebrated French actress, had grown old, she lived in an apartment high above the streets of Paris.

One evening she was visited by an old admirer, who knocked at her door all out of breath from the long climb.

"Madame" he exclaimed, "why is it that you live so high up?"

"Dear friend," replied the actress, "it is the only way I can still make the hearts of men beat faster."

Opportunism

255. Lord Hertford was once asked what he would do if he saw someone cheating at cards.

"What would I do?" he replied. "Bet on him, of course."

256. "How much are the cigars?" asked a customer at the tobacco shop.

"Two for a quarter," said the girl behind the counter.

"All right," said the man. "I'll take one."

"That'll be fifteen cents," replied the clerk.

The customer paid for the cigar and left. A man who overheard the transaction came up to the counter.

"Here's a dime," he said. "I'll take the other one."

Optimism—Pessimism

257. A pessimist sees only the dark side of the clouds, and mopes; a philosopher sees both sides and shrugs; an optimist doesn't see the clouds at all—he's walking on them.

—D. O. Flynn

258. It is told that the administration hired an economist to make a survey and predict what the situation would be fifty years from now. They told him to report back with two projections—optimistic and pessimistic. The months passed, finally his report was read.

"Well, for the optimistic side," he reported, "it is my opinion that in fifty years we will be forced to subsist on crabgrass."

"That's optimistic?" the government expert came back. "What's the pessimistic view then?"

"There may not be enough crabgrass to go around."

P

Persistence

259. A government official in Hong Kong tells the Chinese fable about an old man who had to cross a hill every day. Each day he took a stone in each hand from the top of the hill to the bottom. Asked why, he said, "I'm moving this hill. Not in my lifetime or in my son's lifetime, but in time, this hill will be gone."

—CLARENCE W. HALL

260. After the fall of France, a significant fable was spread in hopeful whispers throughout the stricken country. In its heroic humor was proof of a deep and abiding faith in ultimate liberation by the stubborn people of that country.

The story related that in July 1940, when England faced the enemy alone, Hitler invited Churchill to Paris for a secret conference. Churchill arrived by plane, and was escorted to the Chateau of Fontainebleau, where Hitler and Mussolini awaited him at a tea table beside the famous carp pool.

The Führer lost no time. "Here is what I've got to say to you, Churchill! England is finished. Sign this document admitting that England has lost the war, and all Europe will have peace tomorrow!"

"I regret that I cannot sign it," replied Churchill quietly. "I don't agree that we have lost the war."

"Ridiculous!" exclaimed Hitler, pounding the table. "Look at the evidence!"

Churchill sipped his tea. "In England," he said, "we often settle a difference of opinion by making a wager. Would you like to make one with me? The loser will agree that he has lost the war."

"What's the bet?" asked the Führer suspiciously.

"You see those big carp in the pool? Well, let's wager that the first to catch one without using any of the usual fishing equipment will be declared winner of the war."

"It's a bet," snapped Hitler, who at once whipped out a revolver and emptied it at the nearest carp. But the water deflected the bullets, and the carp swam on undisturbed.

"It's up to you, Mussol" growled Hitler. "They tell me you're a great swimmer—in you go!"

The Duce shed his clothes and jumped into the pool; but try as he would, the carp slipped through his grasp. At last, exhausted, he clambered out empty-handed.

"It's your turn, Churchill," Hitler rasped. "Let's see what you can do!"

Churchill calmly dipped his teaspoon into the pool, and tossed the water over his shoulder. Then again. And again.

Hitler watched open-mouthed. "What on earth are you doing?" he demanded impatiently.

"It will take a long time," replied Churchill, keeping right on dipping, *"but we are going to win the war!"*

—Colonel Rèmy

Perspective

261. A friend called on the English writer, Gilbert K. Chesterton, one day and found him packing his bags for a trip. Since they were old friends, he felt free to ask Chesterton where he was going.

"To Chamberwell," answered Chesterton.

"Aren't you getting absent-minded like the proverbial professor?" chided the friend. "You are in Chamberwell. This is where you live."

"Yes," said Chesterton, "and that is why I am going away. I'm too close to Chamberwell to see it properly. Things have become too familiar for me to notice them."

That is why it is a good thing for the average person to get away from his daily work once a year. It breaks the routine and interrupts old habits. When he comes back with a refreshed mind, he sees his job in a new light, and often he finds he can make little improvements that help him do an even better job than before.

Persuasion—Persuasiveness

262.   Tom Reed, for many years Speaker of the House, was an adroit persuader. At committee hearings he would remain silent until everyone had his say, making notes of the objections. When they were all argued out Reed would say:

"Gentlemen, it seems to me what has been said here can be summarized as follows . . ." and Reed would then give *his* ideas—and sell them.

Physiognomy

263.   Abraham Lincoln was once accused, during a debate, of being two-faced.

"I leave it to you, my audience," he replied, "if I had two faces, would I be wearing this one?"

Point of View

264.   Some years ago, we are told by a European traveler, Einstein was asked whether he preferred to be called a Jew or a German. He replied: "There is an expedition now in the South Seas which will make observations either verifying or discrediting my reckonings. And if they verify my predictions I will be known as a Jew in England and a German in Germany."

265. When Thomas Mann was visiting America for the first time, one of Hollywood's literati abased himself before the novelist, emphasizing that he was nothing, a mere hack, his work not to be mentioned in the same breath with that of the master.

Mann listened with infinite patience and courtesy. But when the party was over, he turned to his host, an old friend, and said: "That man has no right to make himself so small. He is not that big."

266. Humphrey Bogart and Lauren Bacall were in the Stork Club when Harry Cohn, president of Columbia Pictures, walked by their table and whispered a few words to Bogart. The actor turned to his wife and beamed: "The picture's a hit."

"What makes you so sure?" asked Miss Bacall.

"Because Mr. Cohn referred to it as 'our picture,'" Bogart explained. "If it was a flop, he'd have said 'your picture.'"

—LEONARD LYONS

Positive—Negative

267. While traveling through an apple-growing area, a man stopped to watch a farmer spraying his apple trees to prevent codling moth damage to the apples. The man asked the farmer, "How come you're so dead set against the codling moth?"

The farmer replied, "I'm not really *against* the codling moth, but I sure *am* for apples."

Like the farmer in this story, we should direct our actions and energy toward what we are *for*. By doing so, we automatically let others know what we are *against*.

Praise

268. Rossini, the Italian composer, was flattered when he learned that wealthy admirers were planning to erect a statue to honor him.

"How much will it cost?" he asked.

"About ten million francs," was the answer.

"Good heavens!" gasped Rossini. "Ten million francs; why, for five million I would stand on the pedestal myself."

Preacher—Preachers—Preaching

269. The clergyman was preparing his sermon as his small daughter watched.

"Daddy," she asked, "does God tell you what to say?"

"Of course, honey," he answered, "why do you ask?"

"Oh," was the reply, "then why do you scratch some of it out?"

270. A popular young preacher in the early days of our country was a favorite of Benjamin Franklin. When he was accused of preaching other men's sermons, he readily admitted purloining a few points. Although he had drawn good crowds, the church let him go, over the protest of Franklin who said: "I rather approved his giving us good sermons composed by others, rather than bad ones of his own."

271. A young preacher was assigned to a church in Kentucky. He wanted his first sermon to be memorable, and he decided on a fiery denunciation of horse racing. As church let out, one of his deacons rushed to tell him that he was in an area known for its fine horses and that many of his congregation raced their horses.

He took the hint, and on the next Sunday delivered a roaring sermon on the evils of smoking. The deacon was back at the first opportunity to warn the preacher that tobacco was grown in the area, that it figured big in the local economy and that part of his salary came from tobacco farmers.

On the next Sunday, the preacher took out after whiskey. The deacon promptly returned to remind the minister that the town had a distillery, where many of the church members worked.

"Well, what can I preach on?" asked the frustrated young minister.

"Why don't you," replied the deacon, "preach ag'in them heathen witch doctors. There ain't one of them within a thousand miles of here!"

Precedent—Precedents

272. Many years ago a missionary followed a coolie pack-carrier over a Whangho gorge, looking at the frayed ropes of the bridge with apprehension. But the coolie stepped confidently on the boards with his heavy burden.

"Aren't you afraid that the bridge might collapse?" asked the missionary.

The coolie laughed and shrugged a slow negative.

"Why?" insisted the traveler.

Responded the coolie trudging ahead, "It never has."

Professional Fees

273. In the small country parish, it was the custom for the pastor to kiss the bride. However, one bride from another town didn't like the idea and asked her groom to tell the pastor. Just before the ceremony she asked again.

"I did, darling," replied the groom, "and the pastor said that in that case he would charge only half of the usual fee."

274. A doctor, picking up his car at a garage, was highly indignant at the size of the repair bill. "All this for a few hours' work!" he yelped. "Why, you charge more for your work than we of the medical profession do!"

"Well now," drawled the mechanic, "the way I look at it, we got it coming to us. You guys have been working on the same old model since time began, but we gotta learn a brand-new model every year."

Public Speaking

275. In the ancient days of Greece, Demosthenes sometimes ran into a hostile audience when he wanted to talk about serious subjects. On one such occasion, to stop the hissing and to quiet the crowd, he resorted to this little story.

A young man hired a donkey to carry his belongings from his home to another town. The owner went along to take the donkey back again when its task was done. At noon they stopped to eat and to rest. The sun was hot. The owner of the donkey appropriated the shade the animal made, saying that he only rented the donkey and not his shadow. The youth began wrestling with the owner, trying to push him away so that he could occupy the shade himself. All the time the youth protested that when he rented the donkey he rented everything that belonged to the donkey.

Desmosthenes stopped talking and turned to leave, but the crowd demanded that he continue the story and settle the fine point of who was entitled to the donkey's shadow.

At this the famous orator exploded. He shouted, "How foolish can you people be to get so concerned about a donkey's shadow when you care so little about matters of great importance to you?"

Q

Quality

276. During prohibition days, a lawyer was given a bottle of whiskey by a client who had been traveling in the South. It was a brand unknown to the lawyer and, being a little dubious about it, he passed it on to the elderly elevator operator in his office building.

Several days later he asked the operator, "Was the whiskey all right?"

"Just right, sir. Just right."

"Well, what do you mean 'just right?' "

"Sir, you see," was the frank reply, "if it had been any better you wouldn't have given it to me. And if it had been any worse, I couldn't have drunk it."

R

Repentance

277. In 1812 an English Quaker was disowned for marrying a Unitarian. It is reported that he was readmitted after having made a declaration to the effect that, though he could not—out of courtesy to his wife—say that he repented having married her, he could say that he would not do it again.

Replacement

278. When Thomas Jefferson presented his credentials as United States minister to France, the French premier remarked:

"I see that you have come to replace Benjamin Franklin."

"I have come to succeed him," corrected Jefferson politely. "No one can replace him."

—JOHN F. PARKER

Reputation

279. An Irishman in Kansas was brought before the judge for a petty offense. The judge asked the Irishman if anyone present could vouch for his character.

"To be sure, your honor, there's the sheriff."

The sheriff looked amazed. "Your honor, I do not even know this man."

"Your honor," came back the Irishman, quick as a flash, "I've lived in this country for more than twelve years and the sheriff does not know me yet. Isn't that a character reference for you?"

Resourcefulness

280. It is said that Emerson visited a farm one day and was amused to see a boy from a nearby city trying to put a calf into the barn. He shoved and the calf shoved. When he pulled, the calf pulled the other way. A farm girl standing nearby smiled, walked over and put her middle finger into the calf's mouth and gently led it into the barn.

281. Dr. Ernest Dale, New York educator and business counselor, told a convention how an old man in a village once handled a group of young men who were jealous of his wisdom and decided to trap him. The youths planned to show him a bird and ask the old man whether it was dead or alive. If he said it was dead, they would let it fly. If he said it was alive, they would wring its neck to prove the old man wrong. They approached him and asked:

"Old man, is the bird dead or alive?"

"Young man," he said after a long pause, "it is in your hands."

282. When George Bernard Shaw received the Nobel Prize for literature in 1925, people from all over the world wrote to him, asking for financial assistance. The letters all stressed the same theme; now that he had come into a fortune, he could afford to help those in needier circumstances. To discourage the writers, Shaw let word leak out to the press that he had returned the prize money.

Instead of relieving the situation, the number of letters increased sharply. Surely, they argued, if he could afford to return such a fortune, it should be no sacrifice at all for him to help other people less fortunate.

283. It was not that the science professor was a deliberate longhair. He simply forgot that barbers existed until he was reminded of it. This meant that haircuts might be anywhere from three weeks to three months apart.

His students organized a betting pool. Each time the professor's hair became long enough to need a trim, a jar and a piece of paper were placed on a table in the hall. A student would drop in a quarter, sign his name and write his guess for the date of the next haircut.

The professor was greatly puzzled by the mysterious jar and the list which appeared, disappeared, then reappeared in a few weeks. Reacting to his scientific training, he began to keep notes, and after several months the light dawned.

He walked up to the table, deposited a quarter, wrote his name and the date on the list, went to the barbershop, and then returned to collect the pot.

S

Scarcity

284. On a journey to Hanover, King George I stopped at a village in Holland for a short rest. While fresh horses were being readied, the King asked for two or three eggs, which were brought to him. The charge was two hundred florins.

"Eggs must be scarce around this place," said the King.

"Pardon me, sire," smiled the innkeeper. "Eggs are plenty enough; it is kings that are scarce."

The King smiled and paid.

Sculpture

285. The sculptor of the recumbent marble statues of King Ferdinand and Queen Isabella, over their tombs in the cathedral of Granada, in Spain, had a subtle way of trying to show that the Queen was more intelligent than her husband.

There is a deeper depression in the marble pillow on which her head rests, indicating a greater brain.

Self-Employment

286. A young man, tired of working for others, went into business for himself. Later, a friend asked him how it was to be his own boss.

"I don't know," he replied. "The police won't let me park my car in front of my own place of business; tax collectors tell me how to keep my books; my banker tells me how much balance I must maintain; freight agents tell me how my goods must be packed; customers tell me how my goods must be made; federal, state, county, and local agencies tell me how to keep records; the union tells me who I can work, and how and when; and on top of that I just got married."

Self-Help

287. When Andrew Carnegie offered to build a library for any English-speaking community, he enunciated a principle of philanthropy that is one of the cornerstones of the modern Carnegie Foundation.

"You cannot push anyone up a ladder unless he is willing to climb a little himself," Carnegie pointed out. And, true to this dictum, he insisted that any community for whom he provided a library should contribute ten percent of the cost as a maintenance fund.

Help for those who help themselves was one of the principles laid down by the great 19th century industrialist.

—HENRY T. HEALD

Self-Sacrifice

288. The dedication of men of the cloth who serve and lead their fellow men is a blessing to mankind. It was never better illustrated than by the sacrifice of the four chaplains during World War II.

On the *Dorchester*, a United States transport sailing off the coast of Greenland, were a Jewish rabbi, a Catholic priest, and two Protestant ministers. A casualty of war, the ship was torpedoed and began to sink. There were not enough life belts for all the soldiers.

The four chaplains took off their life preservers and handed them to four unequipped soldiers. Minutes later the survivors saw the chaplains going down into the icy waters with the ship, their arms linked, and their voices raised in prayer.

Their names—Rabbi Alexander D. Goode of York, Pennsylvania; the Rev. Clark V. Poling of Schenectady, New York; the Rev. George L. Fox of Gilman, Vermont; and Father John P. Washington of Arlington, New Jersey.

Serendipity

289. Failure in one thing often leads to outstanding success in something else.

More than a century ago there was a young chemistry instructor named William Perkins at the Royal College of Science in London. He used his spare time in a home laboratory to experiment with coal tars. He was searching for a way to produce a synthetic quinine, since the natural drug made from the bark of the cinchona tree had to be imported from South America and was unduly expensive.

One evening, after a whole day of futile labor, he had only a beaker of dirty aniline oil to show for his efforts. For some reason, perhaps to make the vessel easier to clean, he decided to dilute the oil with alcohol before tossing the mixture into the sink. To his wonder and delight, the alcohol changed the colorless oil into a deep, beautiful purple. Unwittingly he had made the first synthetic coal tar dye.

William Perkins failed in his search for a synthetic quinine, but he succeeded in discovering the basis for the great coal tar industry which has given the world innumerable products—dyes, perfumes, drugs, and many others.

Plain William Perkins became Sir William Henry Perkins, on the fiftieth anniversary of his aniline discovery, when he was knighted by King Edward VII in 1906.

Skepticism

290. More than a century and a half ago, when the first American steamboat, Robert Fulton's *Clermont,* was scheduled to make its trial run on the Hudson River, a crowd gathered to watch the spectacle.

One of the spectators was a pessimistic old farmer, who predicted gloomily, "They'll never start her!"

But the steamboat did start. Its speed increased. Faster and faster it went, belching black billows of smoke from its funnel; and the crowd on the river banks went wild with enthusiasm.

But the old farmer turned away, shaking his head, hardly able to believe what he saw.

"They'll never stop her!" he declared.

Speech

291. A young Frenchman in London for the first time was returning by tube from the West End. He put his money down and in his best English accent said: "For Southgate."

He was given four tickets, but thought it was just another strange English custom. At Southgate explanations and a refund for three fares took place.

The next time he traveled he said: "To Southgate."

He received two tickets.

292. The story is told of a number of spirits who demanded admission at the Celestial Gates. The keeper inquired who the first applicant might be.

"It's me," a voice replied. And St. Peter bade him enter.

Another knock. Another question. "Who's there?" Another answer, "It's me."

Finally there came a sharp rap. "Who's there?" demanded St. Peter.

"It is I," a voice replied.

"Another one of those school teachers!" grinned St. Peter.

293. The United States Navy, together with the Speech Research Unit of Kenyon College, once conducted experiments which prove that when a person is shouted at, he usually will shout back even though he does not see the person doing the shouting.

Tests were made using telephones, intercoms, and other devices.

The purpose of the tests was to determine the best tone quality to use when giving orders or commands aboard vessels.

When the first speaker used a soft voice, the one spoken to would answer in a soft voice. When angry shouts were made, the answer would come back in a similar way.

Speed, Relative

294. It took Thomas Gray seven years to write his *Elegy in a Country Churchyard,* but it took Gioacchino Rossini exactly thirteen days to compose the popular opera, *The Barber of Seville.*

Sports

295. Joe Cravath once explained why he preferred running a ranch to his old job, coaching the Southern California football team: "Cattle don't have any alumni."

—S. Perrin

296. The small-time football coach with a reputation for optimism came into the locker room to give the boys a pre-game pep talk.

"All right, boys," he cried cheerily, "here we are, unbeaten, untied, and unscored upon—and ready for the first game of the season."

Superiority

297. The animals were arguing about who had the biggest litters. Some talked about their twins or triplets. Some bragged of a dozen. Finally, they asked the lioness, who quietly replied, "Only one . . . but that one is a lion."

T

Table-Turning

298. Dwight Morrow when once told that someone was speaking ill of him remarked that he couldn't understand why—since he had never done him a favor.

299. When Irvin S. Cobb was 27 years old he went to New York City. With a wife and a sick child to support he started to pound the big city's pavements, going from one newspaper office to another, looking for work. For two weeks he visited and revisited them, but the bosses always sent word that no help was needed.

As a last attempt, Cobb sat down and wrote a letter to each of the editors, proving that he could write effectively and had confidence in himself. The letters ended as follows:

"This positively is your last chance. I have grown weary of studying the wallpaper design in your ante-room. A modest appreciation of my own worth forbids my doing business with your head office boy any longer. Unless you grab me right away, I will go elsewhere and leave your paper flat on its back right here in the middle of a hard summer, and your whole life hereafter will be one vast, surging regret. The line forms on the right; applications considered in the order they're received. Triflers and professional flirts save stamps. Write, wire, or call at the above address."

The next day Cobb was offered four jobs!

Tact

300. Gilbert Stuart, the celebrated portrait painter, once met a lady in the street in Boston, who saluted him with, "Ah, Mr. Stuart, I have just seen your miniature and kissed it, because it was so much like you."

"And did it kiss you in return?"

"Why, no."

"Then," said Stuart, "it was not like me."

301. Victor Borge was playing at the Waldorf when a waiter slipped him a note which read: "Lauritz Melchoir and Jean Hersholt both at ringside."

"I rarely introduce big names from the stage," says Borge, "but in this case, since both visitors were old friends and fellow Danish-Americans, I made an exception. 'I have the privilege of introducing two great Danish artists whose talents have given so much pleasure to millions of Americans,' I said. 'I honestly don't know in what order to introduce them. So I'm sure that Jean Hersholt won't mind if I mention Lauritz Melchior first.'"

Talent

302. A Kansas City newspaper editor studied the sketches handed to him by the young man, then shook his head. Not only did he reject the application for a job, but told the artist he had no talent.

Faith in his own ability led the artist to try other offices, but the results were the same. Finally he secured a job drawing publicity material for churches. The young man rented a mice-infested garage and there turned out his sketches. He also continued to produce free-lance material and eventually his work began to find a market.

Thirty years ago Walt Disney was famous and so was one of the mice in that garage where he had received the inspiration for his Mickey Mouse series.

—Joseph Hutnyan

Taxes

303. A Dutchman was explaining the red, white, and blue Netherlands flag to an American: "Our flag is symbolic of our taxes," said the Dutchman. "We get red when we talk about them, white when we get our tax bills, and blue after we pay."

The American nodded. "I know what you mean. It's the same in the United States, only we see stars, too!"

Time

304. If you had a bank that credited your account each morning with $86,400, that carried over no balance from day to day, and allowed you to keep no cash in your account, and every evening canceled whatever part of the amount you had failed to use during the day, what would you do? Draw out every cent, of course!

Well, you do have such a bank, and its name is "time." Every morning it credits you with 86,400 seconds. Every night it rules off, as lost, whatever of this you have failed to invest to good purpose.

If you fail to use the day's deposits the loss is yours.

305. We speak of saving time and also of wasting it. We say time flies or time drags. And yet we cannot say what time itself is! Our age is one of speed. We are constantly inventing mechanical devices to hasten all tasks and to traverse distances in space with ever-increasing speed. We want to go faster and faster because we want to "save" time.

The story is told of an old Chinese who failed to respond enthusiastically to the glowing accounts of the speed of air travel. He listened unmoved, and then asked: "But what will you do with the time so 'saved?'"

It is not merely saving time that makes for progress, but how we utilize the time saved.

Tit for Tat

306. A prudish lady once accosted the learned Samuel Johnson shortly after publication of his monumental dictionary of the English language.

Said she, "Dr. Johnson, I am distressed that your dictionary contains so many vulgar words."

Replied the gentleman, "Madam, I am immeasurably distressed that you actually looked them up!"

307. Two ministers were walking along a country road. One of them took a cigar out of his pocket, lit it and began to smoke. The other viewed this action with obvious disfavor, and didn't hesitate to say so. "Brother, I see you smoke. I am amazed at you. Are you not aware that it is an inexcusably vile habit? Why, even a pig won't smoke!"

They walked on in silence for a few minutes, and then the smoker uncorked the following reply, between puffs on his cigar: "Brother— I've been thinking of what you just said—about a pig not smoking—and I infer that you mean—to suggest some subtle resemblance—between me and a pig. But, my dear brother—inasmuch as you do not smoke— and the pig does not smoke—it appears to me that there is a greater resemblance between you and the pig—than between me and the pig!"

308. The story is told that in a village not far from Quebec there lived a baker who bought his butter from a neighboring farmer. One day he became suspicious that the butter was not of the right weight, and for several days he weighed the butter and found that the rolls were gradually diminishing in weight. He had the farmer arrested for fraudulent dealing.

At the trial the judge said to the farmer: "I presume you have scales?" "Yes, of course, your honor." "And weights, too, I presume?" "No, sir." "Then how do you manage to weigh the butter which you sell?"

"That's easily explained, your honor," said the farmer. "When the baker commenced buying his butter of me I thought I would get my bread of him, and it is the one-pound loaves I've been using as a weight for the butter I sell. If the weight of the butter is wrong he is to blame himself."

Title—Titles

309. A young girl asked her mother what "vice" meant. Her mother carefully explained it meant doing all sorts of bad things, and then asked why her daughter wanted to know.

"Oh," exclaimed the girl excitedly, "I've just been elected vice president of our home room."

Tradition

310. While touring the south of France by car, a man came to a small town where a brass band of twelve musicians was blaring away in the square outside a house. This puzzled him because all the doors and windows of the house were shut and there was no sign of life there.

During an interval he approached one of the players and inquired: "May I ask why you are doing this?"

"Certainly," was the reply, "we're serenading our burgomaster. It's his birthday. He lives in this house."

Still puzzled, the man then asked the conductor of the band: "Why doesn't the burgomaster come to the window to acknowledge your serenading?"

"Because I have to be down here conducting," the man replied. "I can't be in two places at once, can I?"

Travel

311. A salesman who was growing nervous about traveling by air went to a statistician one day. "Can you tell me," he asked, "what the odds would be against my boarding an aircraft on which somebody had hidden a bomb?"

"I can't tell you until I've analyzed the available data," the statistician replied. "Come back again in a week."

"Well," the salesman asked on his next visit, "do you have the answer?"

"Certainly," the statistician said. "The odds are one million to one against your getting on an aircraft with a bomb on it."

"Those are good odds," the salesman mused. "But I'm not sure they're good enough for me. I travel a good deal."

104

"Well, if you want to be really safe," the statistician said, "carry a bomb with you. The odds are one billion to one against your boarding an aircraft with two bombs on it."

Truth—Truthfulness. See also Veracity

312. A fisherman insisted it was time to start fishing even though his wife protested that he wouldn't catch anything. On his way home after a day of hard luck, he went to a fish store and said to the clerk, "Just stand where you are and throw me five of the biggest fish you've got."

The clerk could hardly believe him and demanded, "Why throw them?"

The angler replied, "So I can tell my wife I caught them. I may be a poor fisherman but I am no liar."

313. The man who does not tell the truth is likely to be found out. As in the case of the country clergyman who said to his flock:

"Folks, the subject of my sermon this evening is 'Liars.' How many in the congregation have read the 69th chapter of Matthew?"

Nearly every hand in the congregation went up immediately.

"That's right," said his reverence. "You're just the folks I want to preach to. There is no 69th chapter of Matthew."

314. The captain wrote in the ship's log: "First mate was drunk today."

After sobering up, the mate went to the captain and pleaded with him to strike out the record.

"It was the first time in my life I've been drunk," he pleaded, "and I promise never to do it again."

"In this log we write only the truth," stormed the skipper.

Next day it was the mate's turn to keep the log, and in it he wrote: "Captain was sober today."

Turnabout

315. When in the United States, Dr. Wu Ting-fang, the grand old man of the Chinese diplomatic service in his day, was questioned sweetly by an American:

"What 'nese' are you—Japanese, Javanese, Chinese?"

Replying that he was Chinese, he asked in turn: "and what 'kee' are you—monkey, donkey, or Yankee?"

—L. Z. YUAN

316. At a dinner some years ago in honor of the then newly elected president of the University of Chicago, Dr. Robert M. Hutchins, a visiting educator who did not know the young president remarked to the lady at his side, "So that is the new president!"

"I beg your pardon, but do you know who I am?" the lady asked stiffly. The visiting dean admitted that he did not. "Well," she remarked icily, "I am Mrs. Hutchins."

The stranger was stricken dumb for a moment, then said, "I'm sorry. Do you know who I am?" Mrs. Hutchins shook her head.

"Thank God," the dean responded weakly.

—MILTON BACON

317. Mark Twain met a friend at the races one day in England who complained he was broke and asked Mark to buy him a ticket back to London.

"Well," Mark Twain said, "I'm nearly broke myself, but I'll tell you what I'll do. You can hide under my seat and I'll hide you with my legs." To this the friend agreed.

Then Mark went to the ticket office and bought two tickets. When the train pulled out, his friend was safely under the seat. The conductor came around for the tickets and Mark gave him two. "But where is the other passenger?" the conductor asked.

Tapping his head, the humorist said in a loud voice, "That is my friend's ticket! He is a bit eccentric and enjoys riding under the seat."

U

Unanimity

318. One day a rent collector returned three times to knock at a certain house, each time without getting a reply. Becoming enraged, he went back a fourth time, and in response to his knock an urchin opened the door.

"Where were you all day?" demanded the collector.

"I was out," replied the boy.

"Where is your father?"

"He's out."

"Where is your mother?"

"She's out."

"Well," said the collector, "I'll just go in and sit at the fire until some one of them returns."

"But the fire's out, too," quickly responded the boy.

Uncertainty

319. Ancaeus, King of the Leleges in Samos, planted a vineyard; so heavily did he oppress his slaves that one of them, it is said, prophesied to him that he would never live to taste the wine from the grapes. When the wine was made, the king sent for his slave, and said, "What do you think of your prophecy now?" The slave made answer, "There's many a slip 'twixt the cup and the lip." The words were scarcely uttered when Ancaeus was informed that a wild boar had broken into his vineyard, and was destroying it. Ancaeus, setting down the cup untasted, hastened to attack and drive out the boar; but he was killed in the encounter.

Understanding

320. Mrs. Albert Einstein was asked one day if she understood her husband's theories. She replied: "I understand the words, but I don't always understand the sentences."

321. Seems that the late Adlai Stevenson was being taxied to the airport one day and introduced himself and started passing the time of day with the cabbie.

"People say I talk over the heads of the average man," Mr. Stevenson said. "What do you think?"

The cab driver pondered the question. Then, "Well, Governor, *I* understand you, but I'm not so sure about the average man."

322. During a heated discussion at a board meeting of economic conditions, one member sat quietly serene amid the furious argument and table-pounding.

Later he was told by the chairman, "I want to compliment you. How did you manage to keep so cool in there when everyone else was blowing his top?"

"Well, sir," replied the serene member, "I simply didn't understand what everyone else was talking about."

Unity

323. A husbandman who had a quarrelsome family, after having tried in vain to reconcile them by words, thought he might more readily prevail by an example. So he called his sons and bade them lay a bundle of sticks before him. Then having tied them up into a fagot, he told the lads, one after another, to take it up and break it. They all tried, but tried in vain. Then, untying the fagot, he gave them the sticks to break one by one. This they did with the greatest ease. Then said the father: "Thus, my sons, as long as you remain united, you are a match for all your enemies; but differ and separate, and you are undone."

—AESOP

Usefulness

324. When French author Anatole France received the coveted cross of the Legion of Honor, he was still a poor man, having earned little from the sale of his books. His friends were bitter about the award.

"Why didn't they give you a cash prize?" protested one of them. "This serves no useful purpose."

"Oh, I wouldn't say that," said France, more philosophical. "When I wear the sash, it will cover the stain on my jacket. That's useful."

V

Vacation—Vacationing

325. Two girls employed in the Chicago Stock Yards went on a vacation to a famous Wisconsin resort. One day they set out for a mystery drive by motor coach. This proved to be a run to Chicago, and included the privilege of being shown through the Stock Yards.

326. Mother was in the habit of taking her annual holiday abroad, while father took his in the form of shooting expeditions nearer home.

This worked well until a few days before her return mother sent the customary telegram home to father to stock the larder.

She wrote on the telegraph blank: "Home Saturday. Be there." Father received the following telegram: "Home Saturday. Beware."

327. One summer evening, when Thomas A. Edison returned home from his work, his wife said, "You've worked too long without a rest. You must take a vacation."

"But where will I go?" he asked.

"Decide where you'd rather be than anywhere else on earth and go there," was the answer.

"Very well," promised Mr. Edison, "I will go tomorrow."

The next morning he returned to his laboratory.

328. "Where's Schemer? I haven't seen him for a long time." "On vacation."

"Again? He just had a vacation a few weeks ago."

"That was unused time from last year's vacation."

"I see. What's he using now? Time he has coming from this year's vacation?"

"No. He's saving that for the end of the year. To work in with the holidays."

"But what's he using for this vacation?"

"He borrowed a week from next year's vacation. What's wrong? You look confused."

Value—Values

329. Oscar Levant is said to have once asked George Gershwin, "Tell me, George, if you had it to do all over, would you fall in love with yourself again?"

330. La Gabrielli, a celebrated singer, having asked 5,000 ducats from the Empress of Russia as her fee for singing at St. Petersburg for two months, the latter replied: "I pay none of my field marshals on that scale." "In that case," said La Gabrielli, "Your Majesty has only to make your field marshals sing." The Empress paid the 5,000 ducats without further demur.

—SEBASTIAN CHAMFORT

331. An English newspaper once carried this gossip item: "James McNeill Whistler and Oscar Wilde were seen yesterday at Brighton, talking as usual about themselves." Whistler clipped the item and sent it to Wilde with a note saying: "I wish these reporters would be accurate. If you remember, Oscar, we were talking about me." To which Oscar sent the following telegram in reply:

"It is true, Jimmie, we were talking about you, but I was thinking of myself!"

332. A family had just moved to a small town in New England and after finding a house to live in, the woman of the family was familiarizing herself with the local stores. Intent on getting some meat for her family's evening meal, she entered the only meat market in the village and was surprised to find only two trays of meat in the showcase. Upon closer examination, she found that the meat looked exactly alike to her.

"How much is this meat?" she asked, pointing to one of the cases.

"Fifty cents a pound," replied the old butcher.

"And that?" she asked, pointing to the other tray.

"One dollar a pound," was the reply.

"What's the difference?" she asked.

"No difference," grunted the butcher. "Some people like to pay fifty cents a pound, some like to pay a dollar!"

333. "I witnessed an amusing incident at one of the local theatres the other evening," remarked a theatre-goer. "A woman wearing a large picture hat was seated directly in front of an elderly man, who was straining his neck in an endeavor to see what was happening on the stage and, of course, it was possible for him to see but one-third of the performance.

"The second act had begun, and I could plainly see that his anger was increasing. At last, when he could stand it no longer, he lightly tapped the woman on the shoulder and in as gentle a tone as he could muster said:

" 'Madam, pardon me, but I paid two dollars for my seat, and your hat . . .'

" 'My hat cost twenty-five dollars, sir-r-r,' came the haughty reply.

"The conversation was at an end."

Veracity. See also Truth

334. Heywood Broun was listening with disbelief to a speaker at a political rally who was giving his own version of the facts.

"How does he get away with it?" whispered a fellow reporter to Broun. "He's murdering the truth."

Broun shook his head in disagreement. "He'll never get close enough to it to do it bodily harm," he said.

335. A Hollywood producer got in early one morning to find his wife awake and raging. "Where have you been?" she demanded.

"Well," the producer explained, "we previewed my new picture, and then I got to talking to the leading lady—a very lovely person. We went to a restaurant, had a few drinks, and then she said she'd like me to see her to her apartment. Well, you know how it is—one thing led to another, and here I am."

"Now don't you lie to me, you horrible creature!" screamed the wife. "I know you've been out all night playing poker with the boys!"

336. A New Yorker, pointing to a hillside field, complimented the New Englander on his corn.

"How do you plow that field? It looks pretty steep."

"Don't plow it; when the spring thaws come, the rocks rolling down hill tear it up."

"That so? How do you plant it?"

"Don't plant it really. Just stand in my back door and shoot the seed in with a shotgun."

"Is that the truth?" asked the New Yorker.

"Hell, no. That's conversation."

Verbosity

337. Justice Felix Frankfurter once wrote a dissenting opinion in which he used the phrase "one word more remains to be said," and then went on to write twenty more pages—plus a sixty-two page appendix.

338. *Professor:* "I say, your tubular air container has lost most of its rotundity."

Motorist: "Says which?"

Professor: "The cylindrical apparatus which supports your vehicle is no longer inflated."

Motorist: "I beg your pardon . . ."

Professor: "The elastic fabric surrounding the circular frame whose successive revolutions bear you onward in space has failed to retain its pristine roundness."

Little boy (coming to the rescue): "Hey, mister, you got a flat tire."

339. A minister of the gospel found himself without a position, and hearing of a congregation which lacked a preacher, he made application for the position. When asked for references, he gave the name of one man at his old church who had been kind to him, hoping to keep the Board to which he was applying from finding out too much.

Back came the letter of recommendation from the man he had given as a reference, and when the letter was read aloud to the Board of Deacons, it seemed wonderful. It said:

"The young man is a fine student of the Word, an accomplished speaker, a good organizer, and a good mixer. He is faithful and zealous in his church work."

If the letter had stopped there, the young preacher would have certainly had a job quickly. But it continued:

'Only one possible criticism could be made of the young man, which is that he is loud-mouthed and quarrelsome when he's drunk."

Vice Presidency

340. For many years there hung in the President's office in the White House an elaborate crystal chandelier which had been bought in Paris by Thomas Jefferson.

It remained more or less unnoticed until Theodore Roosevelt came into office. T. R., an outdoor man who loved fresh air, usually worked with the windows open. The breeze blowing in caused the prisms to tinkle. For some time Roosevelt endured this distraction—with mounting impatience. Then one day he growled, "Get this thing out of here."

"But, Mr. President, where shall we put it?" he was asked.

Roosevelt thought this over for a moment.

"Put it in the Vice President's office," he ordered. "He has nothing to do anyway. Maybe it will keep him awake."

—E. E. EDGAR

Victory

341. College alumni who take such fierce pride in the prowess of their alma mater's football team could well heed the words of one of polo's great players, Devereux Milburn, who said: "It is nonsense to say that the 'will to win' is all that matters. It is the battle—the contest—that counts, not the score. If two meet, one must win and one must lose. But they can both have a great afternoon."

Vision

342. Some years ago, in a Federal courtroom in New York, a sardonic district attorney presented to a jury a glass gadget which looked something like a small electric light bulb. With masterly scorn he accused the defendant of claiming that by use of this "worthless" device, the human voice would some day be transmitted across the Atlantic. He said that gullible investors had been persuaded by such preposterous claims to buy stock in a company and urged prison terms for the defendant and his partners. Two of the associates were convicted, but the inventor got off with a severe lecture from the judge.

The defendant in this case was Lee de Forest; the "worthless glass bulb" was the audion tube, greatest single invention of the 20th century and the foundation of today's four billion dollar electronics industry.

—HARLAND MANCHESTER

Vocabulary. See also Language

343. A visitor to the poet Wordsworth asked the servant at the door, "Where is his study?" "Here is his library," was the answer; "his study is out of doors."

344. Thomas Babington Macaulay, when only four, had an amazing vocabulary. Taking coffee in a great lady's house one day, he was severely scalded when a cup was upset. His hostess fussed a good deal. Putting her arms around Thomas, she tried to console him, using baby language, until the future historian astonished her by saying, "Madam I thank you, but the agony is now abated."

345. A foreign gentleman got into a taxi and looked appealingly at the driver. "I haven't much good English," he began brokenly, "and I've lost the word."

"You mean you've forgotten the name of the street where you want to go?" asked the driver.

The man nodded, tapping his head vigorously as though to shake the missing word loose. Finally he smiled and said, "Take me to the wife of king street."

The taxi driver lost no time in driving him to Queen Street.

Vote—Votes—Voting

346. A farmer was detained for questioning about an elections scandal. "Did you sell your vote?" the U.S. attorney asked.

"No sirree, not me," the farmer protested. "I voted for that there fella 'cause I liked him."

"C'mon, now," threatened the attorney. "I have good evidence that he gave you five dollars."

"Well, now," the farmer said, "it's plain common sense that when a feller gives ya five dollars ya like him."

347. One vote has many times made the difference, even in national elections. Three of our early presidents were made head of our country by a one-vote margin over their opponents: Thomas Jefferson, John Quincy Adams, and Rutherford B. Hayes . . . One man in history, were he alive today, could tell you what a powerful effect a one-vote margin can have on the neck. King Charles I of England had an appointment with the executioner when the vote to behead him was 67 against and 68 for.

—E. CRENSHAW

Vulgarity

348. A woman once asked Dr. Samuel Johnson if a certain nude painting was vulgar.

"The painting isn't, madam," he replied, "but your question is."

Perhaps he answered the question for all of us. Or, if he were answering the question today, he might say it all depends on what's in your mind.

W

War

349. A German was the guest of a Frenchman who asked him how they distinguish between an optimist and a pessimist in Germany.

"It is very simple," replied the German. "The optimists are learning English and the pessimists are learning Russian."

350. It cost about 75¢ to kill a man in Caesar's time. The price rose to about $3,000 per man during the Napoleonic wars; to $5,000 in the United States Civil War; and then to $21,000 per man in World War I. Estimates for the future wars indicate that it may cost the warring countries not less than $50,000 for each man killed.

—Senator Homer T. Bone

Warning—Warnings

351. "I'd like to bring Bill home to dinner tonight," the man telephoned his wife.

"To dinner tonight!" she screamed. "You idiot, you know that the cook just left, I've got a cold, baby's cutting his teeth, the furnace is broken, and the butcher won't give us any more credit until we pay up . . ."

"I know," the husband interrupted quietly. "That's why I want to bring him. The poor fool is thinking of getting married."

352. The young minister was in the pulpit for the first time and he was a little nervous. He read the text: "Behold I Come." The sermon was to follow immediately, but his mind went blank, and he repeated the text: "Behold I Come," hoping to remember the opening words of the sermon—but with no success. Trying to be nonchalant, he leaned forward as he repeated the text for the third time. Under his weight the pulpit gave way and he landed in the lap of the wife of one of the elders. "I'm awfully sorry," he said much embarrassed. "I really didn't mean for this to happen."

The lady smiled kindly and replied, "Oh, that's all right. I should have been ready after you warned me three times."

Well-Wishes

353. The assistant superintendent of schools broke his leg and was hospitalized. Most of his get-well messages he tossed away after reading. But one he kept. It was a telegram which read: "The Executive Board of the County Education Association, by a vote of 7 to 5, has instructed me to send you its wishes for a speedy recovery."

Will-Power

354. An old Negro preacher once cautioned his flock, "When you're looking at your neighbor's melon patch, brethren, you can't keep your mouth from watering, but you can run."

355. *Minister:* "Should I give you something to strengthen your will-power?"

Parishioner: "No, give me something to weaken my conscience instead."

Will, Testamentary—Wills, Testamentary

356. *Lawyer, reading client's last will and testament to circle of expectant relatives:* "And so, being of sound mind, I spent every damn cent I had before I died."

357. "Where did you get that beautiful diamond stick pin?" Smith asked of his friend who was sporting a two-carat brilliant.

"This?" asked Jones, pointing to the "searchlight" which shone from his necktie. "This is a testamentary stone."

"A testamentary stone! What is that?" asked Smith.

"Well, I'll tell you, it's like this," replied Jones. "A friend of mine died leaving a will. In the will he named me his executor and further provided that his executor should take $3,000 out of his estate and buy a stone to his memory. This is it!"

Wit and Humor

358. When Samuel Rogers told a joke at which nobody laughed, he would say reflectively: "The curious part of that story is that stupid people never see the point of it." Whereupon, of course, everyone laughed uproariously.

359. Actor Sir Cedric Hardwicke listened while a man told a long story. But the man spoke so indistinctly and muffed his punch line so badly that the story wasn't funny. "Why did you laugh?" a friend asked Hardwicke afterward.

"I always do," the actor replied. "If you don't laugh, there's danger of their telling it over again."

360. Charles Lamb once had the misfortune to be seated next to a very garrulous and senseless woman at a dinner party. She chattered incessantly and then, discovering that the author was paying no attention whatever to her, rebuked him by saying: "You seem to be none the better for what I am telling you."

"No, madam," he answered, "but this gentleman on the other side of me must be—for it all went in one ear and out the other."

Woman—Women

361. I have heard Lincoln say he thanked God that he was not born a woman, because he could not refuse any request if it was not apparently dishonest.

—WILLIAM HENRY HERNDON

362. When Beau Brummell was asked the secret of his success with women, he answered: "Oh, I merely treat the charwomen like duchesses, and the duchesses like charwomen."

—MARGERY WILSON

363. A reporter was interviewing Sir Winston Churchill. "What do you say, Sir," he asked, "to the prediction that in the year 2000 women will be ruling the world?"

Churchill smiled his wise, old-cherub smile, "They still will, eh?"

364. A great psychologist was once asked by a lady if he did not think that woman was the best judge of woman.

He replied: "Not only the best judge, my dear lady, but the best executioner."

365. One of the most charming women in society, a peeress, remarked to the former Prince of Wales:

"I wish I could go into business. I should like to decorate houses."
"By living in them Lady . . . ?" asked the prince.

366. A recent newspaper ad for a small college was headed: "Short Course in Accounting for Women."

Not long after it appeared, the ad drew one short letter, addressed to the school's president. "There is *no* accounting for women."

367. A garage man answered the distress call of a woman motorist whose car had stalled. He responded to the call and made an examination. "Your car is out of gas," he stated.

"Will it hurt the car," she asked, "if I drive it home with the gas tank empty?"

368. Dante adored woman; Wordsworth commended her; Shakespeare loved her; Tolstoi planted her in sunshine and watered her with his tears, only to tear her up by the roots at last; Burns smiled at her; Moore succumbed to her; Henry James studied her; de Maupassant thought her wicked, but interesting; Bourget dissected her; Balzac understood her.

369. In the French Parliament, one of the deputies, making a speech urging the improvement of the legal status of women, cried: "After all, there is very little difference between men and women!"

With great accord, the entire Chamber of Deputies rose and shouted as one man: *"Vive la difference!"*

—Milton Wright

370. A lady approached Congressman John Allen, of Mississippi, one day and held out her hand. "Now confess, Mr. Allen," she said, "that you've forgotten all about me."

He had. He knew her face, but his memory would serve him no further. But with a low bow he replied, "Madam, I've made it the business of my life to try to forget you."

—O. Henry

371. An explorer was describing some of his adventures before an audience of women.

"Suddenly I came upon a tribe of wild women," he said, "who, strangely enough, had no tongues."

"Heavens! No tongues?" exclaimed one of his listeners. "How could they talk?"

"They couldn't," said the adventurer. "That's what made them wild."

Wonderment

372. A Navy physician in the Pacific received from his fiancée a snapshot taken on a beach and showing two couples smiling contentedly while his girl sat alone at one side, forlorn and lonely. The accompanying letter explained that this was how she was fretting away the time until he returned. At first the physician was delighted, displaying it proudly to several fellow officers. That night, however, after studying it a long time in silence, he turned to his roommate. "John," he said, "I wonder who took that picture?"

—ROBERT J. DOYLE

Word—Words

373. "Mamma," shrieked the little boy, watching his toy train in operation, "it's faster than hell, ain't it?"

"Willie," exclaimed the modern mother, "how many times do I have to tell you never to use that vulgar word 'ain't?'"

374. A romantic tale lies behind the phrase "sub rosa." According to ancient legend, the Greek god of silence, Harpocrates, stumbled upon Venus, the goddess of love, in the course of one of her amorous adventures.

Cupid, Venus' son, happened along at an opportune moment and,

122

by making a gift of a rose to Harpocrates, bought his pledge of secrecy.

Since that time, the rose has been the symbol of silence.

During the Renaissance and later during the reigns of the pre-Revolutionary kings of France, the rose was a favorite architectural motif and often was sculpted on ceilings of dining and drawing rooms where diplomats gathered.

The obvious implication was that matters discussed "under the rose" were considered to be held in confidence.

—WILLIAM MORRIS

World, The

375. The shipwrecked sailor had spent nearly three years on a desert island, and one morning was overjoyed to see a ship in the bay and a boat putting off for the shore. As the boat grounded on the beach an officer threw the sailor a bundle of newspapers.

"The Captain's compliments," said the officer, "and will you please read through these and then let him know whether you still wish to be rescued."